CHRONICLES OF THE

Widespot Café

DANNEY CLARK

Danney D Clark

DanScribe Publishing

Printed in the United States of America

DEDICATION

Dedicated to all who follow Jesus even when it is difficult
and those who work tirelessly to achieve and advance
God's kingdom here on earth.

ACKNOWLEDGEMENT

A special thank you to a special friend Larry Patrick
without whose editorial, graphic talents, interest and enthusiasm
this work would never have been in print.

INTRODUCTION

In small rural communities there is usually a preferred meeting place where the locals come to share their triumphs and troubles with each other. Sometimes it is the local watering hole, the grange hall, the church, or general store, but often it is the local eatery. Places where they can come, enjoy a cup, tell a story, hear one from a friend, or even a stranger passing through. A comfortable atmosphere where one could bring the whole family or grab a quick bite alone before going home to take care of chores.

Such a place was the Widespot Café. It might have been located in the Idaho panhandle, eastern Washington, or the sparse reaches of Montana; however, whatever the exact location, it provided an unique service as intended by God.

PART ONE

My name is John Roberts, the locals call me "Bum". I am the sometimes cook and full time confidant at the Widespot Café. Pull up a chair and let me pour you a cup while I tell you my story.

God blessed me with what others have called exceptional intellect and has since given me the gift of insight as well. However, like many who receive a gift, I did not appreciate or value it as I should have. An upperclassman, you may have heard of him, and I, founded a little "startup computer company" while at the university that did quite well, allowing me to go wherever and do whatever I wanted for a time. He and I parted friends, he having a vision and me searching to fill the emptiness I felt inside. I accepted a small bite of the apple, $50,000, and a thousand shares of stock as my buy-out.

Nine years went by quickly, I moved from job to job, town to town, never having a close relationship or a feeling of belonging. I worked in every industry, every position, in every field garnering small success but feeling alone and empty inside. To my credit, I lived on my earnings, not touching my investments, but spending all that I made. I drove taxi, waited tables, painted houses, sold shoes, installed computers, cooked, drove truck, did construction, or whatever came along.

Young, healthy, and able to learn quickly, I was easily employable. I have never owned a house, a car, or been married. Like King Solomon, I searched for the meaning of life, and like him, I didn't find it. I had many friends, none close, no ties, few responsibilities, felt no kinship to anyone except possibly the friend and partner I knew in college. But he now had moved on and marched to a different beat.

Then one day I stopped by the Widespot Café intending to just have a meal... that day, it all changed for me. I met Mae and Jib. They were the proverbial ebony and ivory, salt and pepper, the exception to everyone's rule. Mae was fifty-ish, white and squat, standing a shade over five feet with a perpetual smile and twinkling blue eyes. She was outgoing and friendly, generous and caring.

Jib was pushing six and a half feet, black to the point of nearly purple, dark eyes, reserved and deep thinking. Jib, for all his humility, may well have been the smartest man I ever met. Those dark eyes could read a man's soul and offer remedy for its ills.

The Widespot was empty when I came in, breakfast over, with the lunch crowd yet to arrive. Mae sat me down right where you are and poured me a cup without asking.

"How'd ju like yer eggs?" she asked as if it were the most common question in the world. I answered without thinking.

"Jib, scramble two and scatter the spuds with a side 'o ham," she yelled at him. "Whar ya headed?" she asked.

"Can't say," I answered, intrigued with her openness.

"Can't or won't?" she pursued the question.

"Don't now," I answered honestly, "just up the road to see what lies ahead."

Mae looked me over carefully, not rudely, but was very obvious. "You on the run?" she asked again.

"Nope, I have nothing to run from or to," I answered. About then she refilled my cup and turned to the kitchen, "Jib, whar's those eggs?"

"Comin' right up, Mae. He replied, "Is the fella in a hurry or somethin'?"

I answered Jib myself, "no hurry at all, have nothing but time."

Mae smiled, "you youngin's think that you gonna live forever, but your time's a comin' just like the rest of us. When the Lord calls, we all gonna come runnin' no matter who we are or what we doin'.'"

Jib came out of the kitchen carrying a platter of food that'd feed two and set it down in front of me. "You need ketchup or hot sauce with it?" he asked, sitting both in front of me. I thanked him, wondering what the spread was going to cost me and started right off eating. Mae bowed her head and said a little blessing over the food for me, quiet like, not meaning to embarrass me.

"Lookin' fer work?" Jib asked. "We might can find a few days work and a place to stay if you are in the mood." I looked him right in the eye as I ate, could see nothing but an honest man looking back at me.

"Food's good, be pleased to give you a fair day's work for my keep," I answered him, "or I got money if you'd rather."

"You go ahead and finish up, then I'll show you around a little," Jib said, "that gonna fill you up? What do folks call you?"

"My name's John, John Roberts," I answered.

"Mine's Jib and this here is my wife Mae, pleased to meet you," Jib said with a grin.

I had everything I owned in my backpack, with my sleeping bag and extra pair of boots tied to it, never considering or caring how it looked to others. A local, Tom Turner and his wife Hazel came in with their four kids just as I was finishing up. Jib stepped right up and said, "Tom, Hazel, I want to introduce you to Mr. Roberts, he's gonna work for us a spell."

As the lunch crowd arrived, the place filled up with Jib introducing me over and over again to the local folks. Finally, when Mae sent Jib back to the kitchen to rustle up grub for them, I followed. That's how I started cooking and I've been here since. Five years now, and I don't see an end in sight.

I must have looked pretty rough those first few days, hair needed cut, had a day or two growth on my face, had on my traveling clothes. Anyway, the locals started calling me "the bum" and later they just shortened it to "Bum". Now I'm Bum Roberts where ever I go.

Here, let me get you a refill. How about a nice piece of hot peach pie with a scoop of ice cream on it? Sure, made it myself last night. Let me tell you now how I came to stayin' on here.

Turned out that Jib was a genuine war hero, fought in Viet Nam, but came back all messed up in the head. They call it PTSD now, mostly it is caused from folks having to do things that go against their nature. That's the way Mae described it. Jib was raised a Christian, believed it and lived it, but in war right and wrong get messed up a bit, men have to follow orders that don't exactly line up with what God teaches sometimes. He came home not proud of being a hero, but feeling guilty, needing God to forgive him. Maybe needing to forgive himself too.

Mae never knew just what it was that bothered him so, he never said. It was Jib who explained to me how our salvation works, how Jesus made it possible for us to live forever with Him in heaven. It was Jib also who knew what could fill the hole in my heart, give my life meaning and value. I'm saved today because he took time with me. No, Jib died a couple of years ago now. Just went to sleep and never woke up. Guess he had a heart attack or something. I found out then that he was ten years older than Mae.

You see that woman and the three kids who just came in, that's Faith Meyers. Her husband worked for the county highway department clearing snow during the winter, did odd jobs the rest of the year, nice couple. They had it hard just making ends meet with her a stay at home Mom, the three girls and all, on one paycheck. He fell off a roof doing a repair and broke his neck this spring and died. Now they have nothing except their faith in the Lord. They come in every day for a couple of meals, Mae lets them sign, like they were going to pay, but don't expect they ever will. Mae helps a lot of folks out that way who are trying to just get by. She knows how it is herself.

I'd been working here only a couple of months when Jib passed. He had handled the financial part of the business as well as cooking and maintenance. Mae just took care of folks, serving, helping with the cleanup and preparation. But then with him gone she found that the café wasn't even breaking even, he'd been using some of their own money just to make payments and keep the doors open.

Our little community here really depends upon the café. The thought of closing the doors kept Mae up many nights before she confided in me about it. I had some investments that weren't needed so I was able to pay off her loan. Guess that makes us unofficial partners, allows her to keep on helpin' folks, and gives me a full time job cooking. You want more coffee?

A young couple came through the door with the look of youthful optimism on their faces. Mae seated them and set down water. "Where you headed?" she asked routinely when the faces were unfamiliar.

"Athol," was their answer, "heard of it?"

"Sure enough, I know folks who live up there, little place up near the Idaho-Canada border."

"We're headed up to see our Grandma, she's been real sick and needs some help around the place."

"Sorry to hear that, where you comin' from?"

"Moscow. This is my twin brother, Ben. He and I have been going to the University there but school's out for the summer."

Mae stayed interested but asked, "Can I get you something to eat?"

"Are your burgers good?"

"Bum thinks so," she answered, giving me a smile. "Bum's our cook."

They ordered two deluxe and cokes which I threw on the flattop to fry, grilled the buns, then sliced tomatoes and onions fresh. We use fresh potatoes for fries, so I put a couple of Idaho's finest through the slicer and into the grease to brown up while Mae filled the coke glasses and took them to the table.

"What's your Grandma's name?" she inquired

"Margaret Price" the young girl answered, "guess folks call her Marge. Used to be a school teacher in Sandpoint."

"I do know her, I always called her Maggie myself, but that's 'cause we wuz friends. You'll tell her Mae from the Widespot said Hi won't you? What's wrong with her health?"

Ben spoke for the first time. "They say she had a stroke, was down a couple of days before they found her. She's in a wheel chair, can't go home alone, they say. Betty and I hope we can stay with her until she recovers enough to fend for herself."

I hit the bell, and received a smile from Mae for my trouble, then saw a little sadness creep in as she realized it was me rather than Jib who did it. As the baskets hit the table the kids closed their eyes and bowed their heads, their lips moving quietly. Mae smiled and encouraged them to eat up as she moved to the table where the little Myers family was still seated.

Momma and three little carrot tops had just finished when she sat down and joined them. "How's it goin' Faith?" Mae asked, concern evident in her voice. "Gettin' along okay?"

Faith smiled a sad smile then answered, "Doin' okay. I got on part-time at the county library but don't start until school begins in the fall. Everyone has been so nice, but we still miss him so much."

"Course you do, I know the feelin' myself," Mae said as she patted Faith's hand. "How 'bout I bring you some ice cream with chocolate on it?" Mae asked turning to the children. They squealed with delight, then looked at their Momma to see if it was alright.

Without waiting for an answer, Mae said, "It's on me" and turned toward the counter.

The bell over the door announced Deputy Sheriff Bill Martin's arrival. As I looked up to see the time, 11:15, I could expect the locals to begin arriving any time. I excused myself from my new friend at the counter and went back into the kitchen to began the prep that I had been delaying, the slicin', dicin', and choppin' that was necessary to run a kitchen alone and provide a meal fast and fresh, the way the aged menus promised.

I like to make soup, it lets my creative juices flow, gives a guy the latitude to get creative and use up vegetables and leftovers before they go bad. The big three... carrots, onions, and celery... were the first to go in, then the white potatoes, garlic, and yesterday's standing rib roast were added to the lentils and beans that had been cooking since morning.

Canned, rather than fresh tomatoes, homemade vegetable stock, salt and pepper finished out the four gallons boiling on the gas burner. Should be ready before noon, God willing.

I looked out and Deputy Martin was studying the menu, like he did every day, as though it were his first time. I could have put his corned beef on rye on the grill the minute I saw him, with onion rings rather than fries, and a side of ranch dressing for dipping, but didn't. I waited until I got the wink from Mae as she dutifully asked, "What'll it be today, Bill?"

By the time I took the order off the carousel, the onion rings were up in the basket and the sandwich ready to turn. I smiled, wondering if Bill ever questioned how he could get his order delivered hot in three minutes.

Mae refilled the cokes for the twins, pouring them into paper to-go cups without being asked. "Anything else?" she asked politely as she laid the ticket on the table, then said, "Stop in on the way back and let us know how Maggie is doing, will ya?"

In the corner booth, Faith and the kids had finished up the ice cream. Tina, the youngest, stood up in the seat and gave Mae a million dollar hug and a sticky kiss on the cheek. I gotta bet that was the best tip she got all week. Faith signed her name across the bill and Mae stuck it into her pocket, to be discarded after they left.

Now I don't want to give the impression that no one ever paid for a meal, plenty of the locals brought by the fruits of their labor... potatoes, onions, lentils, beans, fresh corn, and an occasional side of beef or a fat lamb. Jib let me in on how God had it all worked out the first week I was here. Jib was the best example of a Christian man I ever met.

I tasted the soup, added a little garlic powder, salt, and a bag of penne pasta to the mix before pronouncing it "fit to feed." The seats were filling up, I had three orders on the wheel as the rush began for the day. Mae was clearing tables as she took orders and served drinks, looking like a combination juggler/ballet dancer as she moved between the tables.

Buffy, or Buff, or Buford if one was being unkind, came in the back door, wrapping an apron around his considerable belly as he did. He gave me a nod and went right to work scraping dishes and loading the dishwasher. Buffy was a local man, loyal as a dog, but a little short in IQ. I'd heard that he had crashed his bicycle as a child and had minor brain damage, slowing down his thought processes.

He was our one and only paid employee. Mae gave him room and board, and a hundred a week for his labors. He ate twice that, but was dependable, meticulous in making sure the kitchen, dishes, and silverware were clean and never complained. I liked him a great deal. We spent time together discussing the Bible and playing checkers or fishing. He once made a comment on how the two were alike. I suspect that he wasn't as dim as he appeared.

I handed out a turkey club with the first bowl of soup and noticed that the deputy had been joined at the counter by the local ISP, Tom DeGrange. The Idaho State Police, in their clean black and whites, where the epitome of professionalism, spotless in their uniforms, controlled in their speech, and well trained – some seemed aloof and almost arrogant.

Tom, however, while not sharing crude jokes with the locals, was known as a man with a heart as big as his "Smokey Bear" hat. Partly because he lived in the community, but also because of his deep personal faith, he never failed to choose the road which led to justice with mercy.

He often selected something light off the menu in an effort to minimize his increasing waistline. Today however, he chose the soup and a grilled cheese sandwich, looking for the entire world like a giant child in Halloween costume as he ate. I would have laughed out loud, but settled for a smile instead, then not having to explain myself.

Sadie Hawkins, or Beth Hawkins, or the widow Hawkins, depending upon whom you were talking to, entered and took a table alone. She was a spinster in every sense of the word, being all alone in the world as long as anyone could remember. Old timers argued that she had been married once for a short time, others that she had never been with a man.

One story which supported the widow theory was unkind and not believed to be true, but had been repeated enough to gain credibility. That she had been married a single night and afterward had found that her new husband hanged himself the next morning in the barn. Her family had lived in the area since settlement times, her home built around the turn of the century on twenty prime acres.

It was the subject of discussion by many over the years how she lived and paid bills. No one knew. Sadie ordered her usual... Earl Grey tea, soup and crackers. She often indulged in orange sherbet for dessert.

We usually "hand press" our own ground beef which we purchase from the local butcher shop unless fate has kindly provided us with a donation. The ground is 100% lean to which every morning I add ground pork, chopped sweet onions from Washington state, fine grated cheese, white pepper, seasoning salt, and a hint of paprika before pressing it into a 6 ounce ring for cooking. I had several cooking while I topped the toasted buns with condiments.

Like most things, there is a kind of a drum beat to cooking, a rhythm, an order or progression, which makes things come together well. As I fell into it, my production increased and the toil became one of joy. Likewise, I suppose, my ballerina Mae, who was talking and serving beyond the window. Some left, others came, Buffy began to bus tables for Mae, taking away dishes and wiping tables with unusual dexterity.

I seldom found it necessary to hit the bell, but often did to help Mae break free of a conversation without seeming rude. I was growing to love that old weathered face, though in a different way than Jib had. Even pushing sixty she had energy, poise, and a vitality that made her seem younger. I noted that officer DeGrange had left a twenty under his coffee cup, four times the cost of his meal. Tom was a good man.

I saw that someone had ordered a couple of milkshakes so I rounded the corner and started them for Mae who had her hands full at the tables. By the time I returned, the burgers were ready to serve, fries were drained and salted. While we were not the musical duet that she and Jib had been, we were anticipating each other in much the same way. It was gratifying getting to know and serve these people.

I told you, did I not, how I came to be known as 'Bum Roberts'? Yes, yes I did, and the more I hear it, the more I like it. It makes me feel humble and appreciate what I have been given here. Maybe there is a difference in the perception by the public between a bum, a pan handler, beggar, vagrant, or homeless person, I am not sure. However, there should be. I think the designation should be based upon attitude and not circumstance, and man is a poor judge. Only God is in a position to judge the value of a man.

No one but Mae is aware that I am not financially as destitute as I look, and only she because of the need to provide the funds to keep the café alive. Once in a great while I may take a dividend check when the need to help out a "worthy" comes along. But usually I am content to live on what I earn, finding that way of life infinitely more rewarding than my previous one.

Did you notice the quick-up sun shades alongside of the parking area when you drove in? In the summer time, local folks will come, set up tables, and bring their wares to swap with each other. Occasionally a tourist will stop and take home some fresh produce or home cooked jams or jellies.

In the wintertime, we open up that over flow area off through those doors and allow them to sell handmade crafts and such. Looks like a church bazaar in there with quilts, scarves, hats, and mittens and sometimes wood or leather work as well. Some folks make enough extra to get them through the winter months when things are slow.

One couple raises alpacas, a timid little animal that resembles a cross between a sheep and llama. I think they originally come from South America. People from all over stop by to get the wool of the little critters, when they are sheared, to use for knitting. A local hand-dyes and spins the wool into skeins, selling them for quite a price.

Most of the local folks are Christians, or pretend to be. But we are kind of at a crossroads with too small a turnout to support a preacher full time at the county church, so sometimes we hold Sunday service right here after serving breakfast. Jib used to lead it when Pastor Jamison from Priest Lake couldn't come. Now I do my best a couple of Sundays a month.

The church itself is real nice, see that picture there? But a preacher has got to eat and raise a family too. We keep hoping that God will send someone and arrange things so we can have someone full time.

Are you saved? What I mean is, do you have a clear picture in your head that Jesus controls your life. Have you given Him the right to do that? Lotsa folks think being good, working hard, and attending church is all they need, but it doesn't work that way. I like to think it is like cookin' a burger, there's some stuff you gotta do before you send it out the window. I can tell you about it sometime if you like.

Mae had sat down with a family and was visiting now that the pace had slowed a bit, still holding the coffee pot in one hand. Buffy had nosed his way into the kitchen, standing there expectantly like a hungry hound. I noticed, but pretended not, then asked, "You gettin' hungry?" Buff seldom asked, but was of course always hungry. He started the day with breakfast no matter what time it was.

"Sure am," he said, "if you have time now."

"Sausage or bacon," I asked, he always had ham. He screwed up his face as if being asked an impossible question, then answered, "Bacon today." He liked it crispy, so I threw on four strips and laid the grill weight across them, beside a pile of grated potatoes and a slab of bone-in.

"How do you want your eggs?" I asked as usual, giving him the right to choose but knowing it was always scrambled with mayonnaise whipped into them. The mayo makes them light. I looked back toward the sink, everything was ship-shape, clean and put away.

Buff might be slow to grasp something new, but once he did, no one had to look over his shoulder to make sure it was done right. I turned the bacon and replaced the weight, flipped the spuds and ham, and dumped the four eggs on the grill with season salt, and finely chopped bell peppers and onions in them. Buff liked to add his own salt and pepper. I grabbed a platter as the toaster popped up and began loading it while he buttered his own toast.

"Orange or apple", I asked as Buff seated himself at the counter. He had taken off his apron and liked to be served just like any regular.

"Orange, large", Buffy answered.

At the sound of his voice Mae looked over her shoulder and smiled at us. Looking down at about a pound and a half of food, Buffy bowed his head and thanked Jesus for His gift and asked His blessings on it. Buffy never drank coffee, choosing copious amounts of milk or juice instead.

"Any jam?" he asked between mouthfuls.

"Think so," I answered. "Let me see what we have". I returned with both homemade raspberry and strawberry. We never use commercial, someone always provides us with either the makin's or the finished product. Lots of wild berries here abouts, as well as folks who raise their own.

I poured myself a cup, leaning on the backboard, watching the activity on the floor. A stranger held up his cup, I nodded and grabbed a fresh pot. Mae, still holding the other, was deep in discussion.

A few always sat around taking refills and visiting but most had left for work or home by 10:30 or so. Mae swept and wiped the tables, refilled the cream and sugars, and straightened the chairs while Buff and I were busy in the kitchen. I am guessing that Buffy will become a fair fry cook some day if he so chooses. He has the knowledge and ability. I think he just fears the pressure of performing during a rush. His attention to detail is amazing.

It promised to be a warm day today so I am thinking that fruit and salads will be popular sides. I have salted water boiling in a pot with three whole chickens in it. I'll give them 30-45 minutes, then drain and let them cool a bit before I bone them out. Chicken is always a favorite of mine since it can be used so many ways and doesn't cost us an arm and a leg. Once I take off the meat, I'll return the rest to the water where it can boil some more and have good stock to use in other recipes.

I usually run things by Mae for her opinion but we nearly always agree. I am thinking that today's special might be chicken salad sandwiches with a green salad, and for those wanting something hot maybe barbecue chicken on a po' boy bun with fries or rings or mashed potatoes. I have four more chickens already cut up that I can deep fry just by dipping them in buttermilk and throwing a breading on them if need be. I try and keep the regular items on the menu to a minimum, to reduce the amount of waste, spoilage, and inventory, but am glad to add specials to supplement it, to give our visitors variety.

As I looked out, I saw Mae had taken a break and was sitting at the counter sipping coffee and reading the local paper, which really isn't local, but from nearby. "How does chicken sound for a special?"

She looked up and smiled at me, "Sounds fine, smells good too."

I fill her in on my other ideas how to use it and she nods and smiles, then returns to the local section of the paper. I can sense she is missing Jib and wishes the message was coming from him.

The bell above the door announced the postman, Don Taylor, who handed several items to Mae. "Any iced tea?" he asked the room.

I handed him a to-go with a lid before Mae had a chance to get off the stool.

"Just finished it," I replied. "Drink it down some and I'll add more ice before you leave." Don smiled and nodded, getting right with the program. It must be hot outside.

"What's the temp, Don?" I asked him.

"I'm guessin' high eighties or low nineties," he answered, "but it's humid today after the rain last night."

Don is graying around the temples and probably pushing fifty. Most of his route is by car, only a few of us get the personal service. He drives a jeep with the steering on the wrong side like it came from England or something. I always wondered how that works if a guy has to pass. Of course I suppose that almost never happens to a mail rig. Don and his wife Nell couldn't have children, tried but finally adopted. Now they are raising three. They are regulars at church, always sitting right up front.

I had just turned my attention back to the chicken when Don came back in from outside.

"Give me a jump?" he asked. "Guess I am about due for a new battery."

Since I don't own a car, I grabbed the keys to Jib's old pickup off the key board and followed him out. Jib always kept a set of jumper cables and a tow strap in the back. We hooked up and Don gave it a try... nothing. When I looked, both battery posts looked like they were covered with blue-green fur. I went back in and returned with a quart of warm water with baking soda in it that I poured carefully over the terminals. I let it bubble for a few minutes, then rinsed the mess off with clean water before reattaching the cables. This time it turned right over.

"I'm no mechanic Don," I told him honestly, "but I think it is the maintenance and not the battery that is the trouble. What it needs is a wire brush and a good cleaning."

Don smiled and thanked me, then left. I knew that he'd never held a wrench in his life and made a mental note to finish the job for him next time he stopped by. Some folks just never see the need to maintain or check things over, guess that's why God created friends.

"Phone!" Buffy yelled out the side door. I took the call and placed the week's order for milk, eggs, and fresh vegetables, making a plan to check the meat and give Al at the butcher shop a call later. Since we had freezer space I tried to plan and order a week ahead, cooking the fresh first then supplementing it from the freezer as the week wore on.

Tomorrow was Friday and although most locals were not Catholics, many also looked forward to an occasional seafood dinner on Fridays. With the red meat, pork, and chicken, Al was able to send me four whole fresh salmon just in from Washington state. I made a plan to barbecue them outside on the grill and serve them up with Mae's fresh sourdough bread and green salad. I called back and added two dozen more lemons to my vegetable order just to be safe.

It was 2:45 when I sat down for the first time – the chicken boned, grill cleaned, and the tables empty. Mae joined me with an iced tea for each of us.

"How about sour dough bread for tomorrow?" I asked her. "I'm plannin' on grilling some fresh salmon, with a green salad, your bread would really finish it off."

She smiled, then nodded. "How many? I can do bread or rolls, which would you rather?" I knew the rolls were more time consuming so I chose the bread.

The customers loved both. "Maybe a half dozen loaves." She keeps a starter all the time so it took only a few minutes to get the makin's together and sit them in the kitchen where it was hot and humid. It needed to raise overnight before it could be finished and baked.

"Can I fix you a sandwich?" I asked. "I haven't seen you eat a bite all day."

"I'm not too hungry," she admitted, "maybe I should have a bite though. Did we have any of that soup left over?"

"Sure, I have a couple of gallons in the walk-in, let me get you a bowl warmed up and a chicken salad together for you."

I missed Jib too and the loss was so great that we hadn't been able to share it yet. We each just suffered alone. Maybe soon God would begin to heal the wound, allowing us to help carry each other's pain. A couple of tourists stopped by grabbing snacks for their kids off the rack or getting a hand dipped cone but no cook orders until nearly 4:00. Al's meat truck pulled up out back and delivered directly into the walk-in for us, his son Blake the driver.

Blake was a senior this year, built like his dad, being recruited already by some of the local colleges for their football program. When he delivered a side of beef, he carried it in on one broad shoulder and hung it up himself in the walk-in. I did not follow football but was involved enough to know what a linebacker was. I took his invoice and paid him cash from the till after he signed off, then offered him a soft drink or ice cream cone. He declined the cone, saying that he was watching his weight, but took an iced tea with him.

After he left, I inspected the salmon and I was impressed with the fact that they had no fishy smell. That, together with color, meant they were indeed fresh. I fileted them off the bone leaving the skin attached, then saved the heads and bones in the freezer to give me a base for the fish stew that was already coming together in my head for the following Friday. 'Resourceful,' that was the word that Jib had used to describe my method of cooking. He had approved.

By 3:30 I had combined the ingredients of my homemade barbe-cue sauce and had it simmering with chicken in it. The rest of the chicken was waiting to be seasoned, then combined with chopped celery, green onions and my mayo mixture over salad or on bread as a sandwich with chips or fries. If I had been a smoker, it would have been a perfect time for a smoke break. Instead, I took a short walk to the cabin out back that I called home, where my dog greeted me with a smile as she opened one lazy eye. I checked her food bowl, and freshened her water before heading back to the café.

Inside, Mae was just seating the first of our dinner guests, the Spellmans. Buck Spellman is a huge man, tall and wide, with a thin ring of grey hair around the perimeter of his great bald head. His head seemed disproportionately large for his body, making him appear like a male bison to me each time I saw him. I imagine the writer of the Paul Bunyan tales must have known someone like Buck for his inspiration. Buck was a rancher, not a farmer. Some often get the two mixed up.

A farmer may raise cattle in addition to his crops, but a rancher raises livestock and will often be the first to tell you so, as though raising crops was somehow below him. Once in a while a rancher is known to cross over the line and raise food for his own livestock, like hay. Well anyway, Buck and his four strapping sons and substantial wife were seated at our table for eight and had it filled with bodies.

Mae handed them their menus, then sidled over to me with a devilish grin, "should I ask Buck if he'd like to try the chicken special?"

I feigned hurt feelings and replied, "What didn't you like my special?"

"Oh, I liked it fine," she said, "but I'll bet the only time Buck ever ate a chicken was whole with the feathers on." We both laughed.

Several times a year Buck or one of his sons would come by with a whole or half beef and just leave it in the walk-in without saying a word about it. Guess he thought that was part of his tithe or something for attending church here occasionally. I always hand-cut the porterhouses when I saw them drive up, at about 1¼ inch thick they each weighed a pound or more. Since I had no bakers ready to serve yet, I put 5 lb of red potatoes in the water as it came to a boil.

"Got any steak left?" was the answer to Mae's yet unasked question of what they'd like to eat.

Mae smiled at Buck then yelled at me, "Buck wants to know if we have any of that old tough Holstein bull left" knowing full well that it had been a young and very tender Hereford steer. Dairy farmers raise Holsteins, ranchers raise Herefords, Angus, Red Durham, or other meat cattle. The boys laughed with their mother while Buck tried to look offended but lost the battle to keep a straight face.

I picked out the best marbled and aged and cut them off the hanging carcass and yelled back at Mae as I placed them on the grill "Well done, right?"

She answered immediately, "yeah, six petite, well done".

The steaks actually beat the potatoes to the plate, being just grayed on one side before being turned to the other. Any rarer and they'd been still eating grass. A platter, not a plate, covered with steak, had barely room for the Texas toast cut liberally from my last loaf of sour dough bread. I used a regular plate to serve the buttered red potatoes and green salad on the side.

Mae had set two pitchers of cold milk on the table and was already returning to refill the first. $200-250 anywhere they served steaks would have been without tip, but of course we charged them nothing for eating their own beef.

"Burned them again Bum," came the response from the table as Buck had finished blessing the food and cut into his porterhouse. Before the meal was over, each plate would have easily a half cup of blood with only a bone left floating in it. The boys served as the line that kept the quarterback from getting sacked before he could hand the ball off to Blake, Al's son, at the local high school.

The twins approached 250 lbs each while their older siblings closer to 300. It would be quite a loss to the program when they graduated. Tom, the oldest, had a scholarship waiting for him at U of I in veterinary medicine, his younger brother likely would play ball, take the education and return to the ranch. The twins, still freshmen, had not declared their future plans. Their mother, a devout Christian, was stout, grey haired, and had a no-nonsense way about her, running the house with an iron hand.

I hoped the cherry cobbler in the oven was about done as I saw them collectively push back a bit from the table and look around like hungry dogs.

"Gonna have to bring you a bigger steer next time, Bum, that barely took out the wrinkles," Buck said. "Got anything fit to eat for dessert?"

"Let me look", I answered. "I remember Mae made an apple pie Monday, should be a slice or two of it left over."

The cobbler was still bubbling as it was set out to cool. I grabbed six soup bowls and a gallon of vanilla ice cream while Mae cleared the table and set out coffee cups all around. I filled the bowls and heaped ice cream on them until they could hold no more, taking them to the table with a smile.

Buck stood and took my hand in his bearlike paw, "Given some time you'll get the hang of this cooking thing," he said with a smile.

The regulars and a couple of newbies came in about 5:00, then more until at about 6:00 we were running full out. I had the Friday special on the white board and received promises of a return crowd the following night when they saw the menu. Buffy had returned and began by helping Mae bus tables before retiring to the dishwasher. We had our hands full providing the hot and fresh per our promise to the hungry tribe.

The barbecue chicken was a hit, served on a bun or over steamed rice, but with several of the women preferring the salad. Kids, however, wanted the deep fried chicken with fries almost exclusively, causing me to ask Buff to give me a hand with the breading of it.

By 7:00, all that remained was to lock the doors behind us, until a knock on the window revealed Deputy Martin at the front door. I unlocked it as he stepped inside facing Mae and I with a tired face.

"We had a roll over down at milepost 314, a family from out of state. Quite a mess. No one is badly hurt but now they've got no car and little money with no place to stay for the night. Man and his wife and two little ones.

"Bring 'em here Bill," Mae said, "we'll make do, get them a hot meal and a place to stay for the night."

"You sure?" Martin asked.

"Sure, can't see it being a big deal, I'll get a cabin ready for them."

Mae and Buff left the café heading for one of the six small cabins that had once been used as overnight accommodation by a former owner. Buff and I each occupied one, leaving the four to use for dry storage or occasional guests like these. They were occupied more often in the winter when they were needed as someone broke down or got stuck in the snow during a heavy storm. We all pretty much had our hands full with the café, giving us little desire to run a motel.

About an hour later Bill showed up with a thirty-something man, his wife, and two little boys. They were all dirty, tired, and hungry but sported only a few bandaids that Bill must have applied at the scene. From the sound of things, both boys were belted in the back seat and had been asleep when the car had overturned. The wife, Becky, still looked dazed, as though the ordeal was not real. I wondered if the considerable bump on her forehead might be a sign of a concussion. I took Bill aside and posed my fears to him, he promised to come back with Sally, his wife, who was a nurse, and let her take a look.

Mark, the husband, was embarrassed and humble, admitting that he had probably dozed off and over-corrected when he awoke. They had left Calgary early this morning, hoping to get to Moscow where they had family to stay with.

Mae returned with Buff in tow, offering to help them with their luggage and leading them outside toward the cabins. I fired the grill up and turned the deep fryer back on. Mae returned to report that they were cleaning up and getting squared away before returning to eat. Buffy had gone to his cabin for the night.

"Any idea what to fix for them?" I asked her.

She smiled like a grandmother, "I asked the little ones what they liked, they like tomato soup and grilled cheese sandwiches with pickles."

I opened a Campbell's tomato soup that I had around for such occasions, then made a brown gravy and mashed up the remainder of the red potatoes left over from the Spellman family. Then I cut a single big round steak from the side and abused it with the meat hammer before dipping it in egg, then rolling it in seasoned Panko coating.

The flattop was back up to temp, so I put the steak on to brown, before turning off the deep fryer for a second time. Fresh broccoli was steaming right alongside of the soup when the family entered through the rear door, looking tired but clean. The grilled cheese joined the steak as they sat down.

I feared the little ones might doze off before being fed so I asked for permission to serve them first. The boys were tow-heads, four or maybe five, curly hair and blue eyes like their parents. I turned the sandwiches and the chicken fried steak at the same time, then filled two bowls with Campbell's best.

Mae served the children their soup and sandwiches together, splitting a small chocolate shake between them while I plated the mashed potatoes, broccoli, and steak before ladling the gravy over it. There were tears in his eyes when Mark blessed the food and thanked Jesus for protecting them.

Mae and I retired to the kitchen where we had another iced tea while I bricked the grill again and put things away. She filled me in on their story. They were Canadians who were on holiday, coming to visit family living in Idaho. Money in short supply, they had hoped to not bear the expense of food and an extra night's lodging, so they had attempted to drive through. That proved to be a mistake.

The deputy finally returned with the tow truck driver, their car on the rollback. Mark and I walked outside with them to access the damages. It was readily apparent that the ten-year-old SUV was a total loss with the frame tweaked, top caved in, and all the glass broken out in the roll over. Mark looked like a man who had just received a death sentence, a look of despair coming over him.

"I have no insurance for collision," he declared. "We needed to save some money so we took it off as soon as the bank was paid off."

Doug, the tow truck driver, offered his opinion. "I can let you off with $45 if we can leave it here. It'd cost you another hundred to tow it to a shop."

Mark looked at us hopefully. "Is there somewhere we could leave it until we have time to figure it all out?" I nodded, then pointed to several like it lined up in a back corner of the lot.

"Put it over there, would you Doug?"

After Mark and Bill had turned and started back in, I handed Doug a fifty and let him keep the change.

Inside, Mae had bussed the table and was ushering the young wife and her two boys out the back door toward a cabin. I watched as Mark joined them and had a short conference with Becky, who then began to dig in her purse.

I interrupted her, "The tow is taken care of, just try and get some rest."

I could see the tears of frustration and happiness mingling together, rimming her eyes as she smiled and thanked me.

Potatoes were boiling for hash browns, the griddle was hot, and I had the coffee already in my cup when Mark knocked at the back door. I asked him in and offered him a cup while I turned up the oven for Mae's sour dough bread and began spreading seasoned mayonnaise on the salmon filets for grilling later on.

"How'd you sleep?" I asked him.

"Not well," he admitted. "Spent most of the night wishing I could do it over, worrying about how we'd get home, things like that."

I nodded, "That seems about right to me, a man feels the responsibility for everything that happens to his family, and looks for ways to fix it."

We visited for a time before he told me that he was a pastor of a little church in Canmore, Alberta.

A 'new plant' he called it, with only a few dozen couples attending regularly and most of them young and struggling financially like himself.

"The folks you are headed to visit in Moscow, who are they?" I asked.

"My wife's brother and his wife," he answered, "they just got married last year. She's expecting, so we thought it easier for us to travel than for them."

"Seems like God helped you make a good choice," I said. "If they'd been the ones who rolled over, she might have been hurt or even lost the baby."

I could see him trying to see the silver lining in the dark cloud that had wrapped itself around his family. Finally, he smiled and nodded.

Our conversation was interrupted by a knock on the front door. I had forgotten to unlock it and turn around the Open sign. It was Bill Martin, Deputy Martin, who received the distinction of being the first customer of the day.

"Morning," he said to Mark, "how is your family?"

"Still sleeping," Mark answered. "They were exhausted."

"I imagine so," he agreed. "Something like that really eats up your energy once you get over the fear. I spoke to the Sheriff this morning about you. He said we can let you off with an infraction rather than inattentive driving. That's the best we can do where there is a serious accident with damages. It'll be just a flat $25 plus court costs." He handed Mark the ticket.

"You have thirty days to send a check or I'll have to take vacation and come visit you in Canada and arrest you," he said with a smile.

"Thank you," Mark said, obviously relieved to know where they stood.

I refilled their coffees as Mae walked in and joined us, then excused myself to the kitchen. Uncharacteristically, Bill ordered hash browns, bacon, and two scrambled, with toasted English muffin and honey. Mark elected to wait for his family to join him.

After a few minutes Mae came in and stuck three loaves of bread in the oven to bake, as Mark left for the cabin and Bill was finishing up.

"I checked on them 'fore coming over," she volunteered, "the three were sleeping like babies. What are we gonna do about findin' them transportation?" she asked me, just as natural as if we'd been their family.

I smiled, knowing she'd been scheming about it already. "Got something on your mind, Mae?"

"Well," she said, "you know that old Subaru wagon that Buck was trying to sell here last fall and then tried to give the church as a donation without any luck?"

"Yup." I said, knowing the car well, he had bought it for his boys before they began to grow. Hardly owned it before they all outgrew it. It spent most of its life sitting in the barn, in their way.

I smiled, "How much you going to offer him? He was trying to get $5,000 last year, only has 40,000 miles on it he said."

"I'm thinking... it is older now, maybe $1,500 and a dozen meals."

I had to laugh out loud, "Mae, you know he never pays for his meals in cash."

"I know, but he always tips big and donates the beef, besides, he's got a heart of gold and don't need the money."

"Sounds good then, give him a call." I said. "You can take the $1,500 out of my wages." Now it was her turn to laugh. I hadn't taken a paycheck in two years!

Mae checked on the bread, looked at her watch and picked up the phone, ten minutes later she returned to remove the bread with a big smile on her face.

"He said he'd deliver it today with a full tank of gas, but he wants cash, doesn't trust your checks."

I had to laugh, almost seeing the gentle giant smile as he said it. "Most likely if he did take my check he'd never cash it anyway."

Two travelers entered and ordered Denver omelets, juice and

fresh sour dough toast, ate, then left without conversation. Mae put in the last loaves to bake and served a table of six from Post Falls headed to a wedding in Sandpoint, everyone in high spirits and hungry. They promised to stop on their way home. I sprinkled a little dill and parsley on the salmon, wrapped it tightly in plastic wrap and placed it back in the cooler.

When Mark returned with his family, the boys were still rubbing their eyes, but Becky looked rested as they seated themselves in a corner booth. I filled an empty plastic squeeze container with pancake batter, then went out to visit with the boys. They had to show me who Sponge Bob Square Pants and the Octopus were in their coloring book before I could get creative with their breakfast. The boys enjoyed 'cartoon cakes' and crispy bacon with their juice, while Mom and Dad waited for cakes 'n eggs with a side of ham.

With all the fuss last night, I had forgotten to do some baking powder biscuits for the morning crowds' biscuits and gravy and therefore would take a lot of heat for using 'store bought' biscuits. As I was order'n it up and keeping Mae running, I could see Mark talking on his cell phone, to his brother-in-law no doubt, about their circumstance.

As the breakfast crowd cleared out I was running the till while Mae bussed, when Mark approached, wanting to square up with us. I could see he was grimly holding out plastic to me but did not have a ticket from Mae.

"Did you get enough?" I asked, ignoring his card, "able to get hold of Becky's family?"

"Yes, thank you," he answered. "The food was great. Her brother has to work today and their little sedan won't hold all of us so he's trying to borrow something bigger and come down after work. Do you suppose that will be alright with Mae to have us stay in the cabin a little longer?"

I answered, "I think she'd love it, spend a little time with Becky, girl talkin' some."

"Do you fish?" I asked, changing the subject.

He looked startled by the question, but answered, "Yeah, why?"

"I was thinking that maybe you'd keep Buffy company after he gets his chores done this afternoon. He loves to fish and I don't really have time, I have to get ready for a big salmon bake this evening."

Buff hadn't made it in yet, but I knew without asking he'd love to take Mark and the boys down to the little creek and show them his fishing talents. When he returned to the table to visit with his family, I could see smiles all around as he gave me a nod.

I had just finished running a bone-in through the band saw, slabbing it in advance, when Buck and the family came through the door, a grin on his broad face.

"This place got any grub for sale?" he asked. Mae, with the help of the boys, began pulling a couple of fours together to get enough table space for them.

I had 25 lbs of spuds boiled and grated and knew they'd likely use most of them up, so I put on water for more before I left my duties and walked toward the table. I lowered my voice a little, "we haven't had much of a chance to discuss our little deal with the folks who need the car" I said as I inclined my head toward the corner where they sat.

He nodded, then smiled again, "You trying to get out of the deal? A deal's a deal, you got the cash?" I just grinned and handed him an IOU written on a napkin.

"Will that do?" I asked, returning to my chores in the kitchen. It was a little after 11:00 when I served up a platter each of ham, eggs, hash browns, and thick slices of Mae's sour dough toast with their coffee and milk. I poked Mae in the ribs, "we're gonna need another half dozen loaves of bread."

Buffy came in and began the cleanup without speaking. When he slowed down for a moment, I approached him with my idea about a fishing trip. He grinned from ear to ear, and then said, "I got extra gear for the boys, I can dig some more worms too." Then he went right back to work, eager to finish and get to the stream.

I could see that Buck had been keeping an eye on Mark, Becky, and the boys who had finished eating and were sitting visiting, waiting for Buffy to get done. Finally, I saw him stand up and walk over to them, all 9' 12" of him, at least that's how he looked standing over them. He stuck out his bear paw and introduced himself, motioning to his wife and sons still seated.

Then he explained how they came to be here for breakfast this particular morning, nodding toward Mae and I as he did. I could see Mark, at first, shake his head, then as Buck continued to talk, looking up at the big man, tears in his eyes. After several more minutes in discussion, the little family followed Buck out to the parking lot, gathering around the little Outback wagon.

I looked through the window, noticing right away that it had been washed and waxed, by those big sons no doubt, looking like new. Buck's sons followed their mother out and were introduced before giving big hugs and handing Mark the keys, causing smiles all around.

The family headed toward their 'six pack dually' when Buck stuck his head back in the front door. He made a point of showing he folded my IOU and put it in his pocket, then asked what was for dinner. I told him baked salmon, at which he grimaced, then smiled... "and steak? Surf and turf?"

I smiled back, "just for you Buck! The regular folks get the fish."

I started worrying then if I'd have enough food so I called and ordered four more salmon, all they had left. They would not have time to deliver it, so I'd have to find time to pick it up. Friday night was starting to look like a barn burner and I felt like I was running out of time. Not a good feeling.

The breakfast crowd was gone, and lunch had not showed up yet when Mark, Mae and the boys came back inside. Buffy had just finished and was hanging up his apron in preparation to hitting the stream, when I asked him for a favor.

Turning to he and Mark I said, "I am sorry to have to ask you but I need a little help. There's four salmon waiting for me at Al's and they can't deliver today, could you grab them for me before you go to the stream?"

Mark answered immediately, "sure, just show me the way. I need to get used to the new car anyway."

Buff nodded, "I can show you, it's only two miles down the road." Off they went taking the boys with them. Mae and Becky swamped the final two tables and sat together with a glass of iced tea, visiting. Thank you Lord, I said mentally, looking upward as I did.

I took a dozen hands of crispy Romaine lettuce and sliced them into ribbons before covering the two large stainless steel bowls with plastic wrap and replacing them in the cooler. Then I mixed up a gallon of my own recipe Caesar dressing, to add later. Checking, I found I had nearly 10 lbs of Parmesan cheese already grated and ready. I pre-measured two pounds of golden raisins, and one of sesame seeds, then sprayed the croutons with butter spray on a sheet pan and added extra seasonings before re-baking.

With the ingredients ready to combine, the salad was out of the way. I began husking the 15 dozen ears of corn that were in the burlap sack in the walk-in, putting two 8-gallon pots half full of salted water on the burners to heat. It was 12:00 when a few straggled in for lunch wanting burgers and fries, the normal fare. Again I thanked God for the lighter than usual crowd. Becky jumped in and helped Mae without being asked.

The fishermen returned from Al's with the salmon, all smiles before excusing themselves to "get wormy and wet" as the little ones put it. I fileted the new fish, seasoned and prepared them just as their brothers had been, then began slicing lemons on the mandolin.

As the final two guests left the café, Mae joined me in the kitchen and prepared to bake more bread while I checked the charcoal and readied it in the two homemade grills out back. Jib had cut a 55 gallon barrel in half the long way, attached legs, put expanded metal near the bottom to hold the charcoal, then cut some more to fit on the top.

I had about 12 square feet of grill space to use, but what I really needed was another set of hands to help. I missed Jib. I checked my supply of steaks and cut another dozen, noting that I was running low on meat. I then turned down my boiling water to medium to stay hot until needed. Shamefully, I took the lazy man's way out and opened four gallon cans of Bush's Baked Beans, smiling when I remembered the talking dog in the commercial. I wasn't sure that I could improve on their beans anyway.

It was 3:45 in the afternoon when I lit the charcoal. I figured to give it 30 minutes to get ready and then sat down with an iced tea. What had I forgotten? Thank God that this was not an every Friday event, but also that it was to celebrate the blessings that He had provided to the Widespot just that very day. The bread came out smelling wonderful, going on racks to cool, being replaced by five dozen foiled bakers from southern Idaho.

At 4:00 Mark, Buff and the boys showed up, all smiles, holding up a dozen nice-sized native rainbows. Cameras came out of nowhere with everyone laughing and talking at once. Each of the boys wanted to eat their catch, so I cleaned and scaled them, and let them help me season them, placing a tablespoon of lemon butter in each before wrapping them up in foil.

Both Mark and Buffy had donned aprons as had both Mae and Becky, who sat the boys in a booth with their coloring books. I was a little unsure of where to utilize Mark until he told me that he had cooked while in Bible college. I gave him responsibility for the salad, showing him to the components. Buff checked the charcoal and pronounced it "ready" so we began loading the grill skin side down, then covering the top with foil.

I was unsure whether to cook steaks on the flattop or outside until Buff and Mark made it clear they had the fish under control. I relaxed into my rhythm at the grill, saying a prayer for God's blessing over the evening meal, as the guests began to be seated. Outside, Buff and Mark had declared the fish was beginning to "flake", giving sign it was ready to turn. Leaving the skin sticking to the grill, the three of us carefully flipped each filet, placing them back on the skin. Mark and Buff seasoned them liberally with lemon pepper before dousing each with melted lemon-dill butter, then topping them with parsley for looks.

By the time I returned inside, my order ring was full and Mae and Becky were serving up the salad and drinks. I filled a clean sink with hot bakers as the steaks began to fry and sliced the bread, knowing I had no chance of toasting it. The salmon began coming in the back door onto the work counter as everyone jumped in to begin plating. I had forgotten the corn until now, so I added a dozen ears to the boiling water in each pot.

Praise God, Buck was uncharacteristically quiet as he waited with his family and four dozen others for their meals. Mark and Buffy moved with practiced grace around the small kitchen, as if they had done it for years. Mark made a special effort to serve his wife and sons their meal, while not joining them. Both boys promised him a bite of their trout. In all we served sixty meals in an hour setting a record 'personal best' for the Widespot. Jib was smiling down on us and we all knew it.

Yes, I had forgotten dessert. We ran out of ice cream and I heard about it from the jubilant crowd. It was six o'clock when the door was closed and locked with not a bite of salmon left over, our guests already planning for a repeat engagement for the next week. I must have said no a hundred times in every language I know. As Mae was clearing the table, she noticed the usual $50 tip under Buck's plate had been replaced by a napkin with an IOU on it.

Saturday morning came too quickly. At 7:00 we were all still drinking coffee together when someone knocked, asking when we opened. It was our mailman, wanting a little breakfast before setting about his work. And so another day began at the Widespot. Mark,

Becky, and their sons left right after breakfast for Moscow with hugs and kisses and promises to return.

Mae was a step slow this morning while performing her usual ballet but Buffy was beaming and ready for more. I might have been a bit off my game as well, as I prepared two prime rib roasts for the oven, moving mechanically rather than purposefully about the kitchen.

PART TWO

Hello, good morning. Just coffee or can I get you a menu? We haven't met have we, my name's John, but everyone calls me Bum. Sit down and I'll tell you all about it. That is Mae dancing over there from table to table with the coffee and the water glasses, she owns the place. What can I bring you for breakfast? Well, take your time then, we got all the time the Lord allows.

"Morning Tom," I said to Tom DeGrange as he sat at the counter, routinely looking over the folks at the tables. "You got Saturday duty this week?" Tom nodded, "every fifth one now with summer vacations in full swing."

Tom and a small handful of others had responsibility for the state highway from Lewiston north to the border and other associated other criminal activity as well. Many of the municipalities locally were small with little or no law enforcement, depending upon the county Sheriff and the ISP for law enforcement.

Tom and his wife Hazel have only one child, a little girl. Katy must be about ten now. They adopted her when she was a baby after finding they couldn't have children safely. Hazel carries something in the genes that may develop into muscular dystrophy. They didn't want to take the chance. Excuse me, Mae has some orders that I need to attend to.

I went back into the kitchen thinking about what I'd just shared. I had a lot of respect for their decision to both forego their own desire to have children and then for the unselfish one to adopt. Katy is Palouse

Indian full blooded, shows it in her long black hair, skin tone, and cheek structure. She's a bright bulb that lights up the room whenever she enters. I see them some Sundays when we hold the service here rather than the county church down the road.

The wheel was half full, with more coming in, so I stopped my daydreaming and went to work. Short stack and two scrambled, side bacon... ham and eggs over easy, white toast... French toast with cinnamon and powdered sugar, sausage... and so it went until about 10:30 when the locals stopped jawin' and left for their chores.

Buffy was bussing and washing and Mae had finally found her stride and was dancing around the floor as usual, giving refills and wiping tables. When Tom left, his seat was hardly cool when Bill Martin took it. Mae handed him a menu and winked at me, the signal to put on the usual while he pondered his options.

Most folks were still eating breakfast when I put on his corned beef on rye and dropped the onion rings into the hot oil. Faith and the girls were a little late this morning as they took their usual corner booth. I remembered that I had done cartoon cakes for the two boys and moseyed out to see if the girls would like the same. They loved the idea, but came up with characters' names that I couldn't picture, then finally settling for the Lion King characters that were on their coloring menus. Three links and cakes resembling something to which they could relate brought a twinkle to their eyes, and tears to Faith's, who had just coffee and a sweet roll this morning.

I not much of a baker, I leave that to Mae or the commercial guys, finding I am more gifted in other areas. Sometimes Mae will make up cinnamon rolls with the white frosting, but they only last a few minutes with people eating all they can hold before taking them home. We are not really set up to bake and store a lot of raised goods. Cakes, pies, and bread about take up both her time and our extra space. The stranger whom I had greeted a half hour ago finally decided and Mae added his choice to the wheel, now nearly empty. Short stack and one egg, sunny side up. Pretty scant vittles for a grown man. As I sent out the final orders, including his, I looked at him carefully. He seemed nervous, didn't talk to anyone and kept his head down while eating.

Now I'm not a mind reader or anything but a student of human nature, educated by living life among its best and worst. I remembered when I first came to the Widespot, what Jib had asked me... "you on the run?" This guy looked like he was on the run.

I remembered how uncomfortable he had acted when Tom had sat down, and now Bill was sitting in the same chair right beside him. I took out my cell phone and clicked a couple of head shots without his notice, then walked out the front door and did the same to the few vehicles remaining in the parking lot. A blue sedan with Michigan plates was the only out-of-state one in the lot. I snapped its plate before going back inside.

I'm the first to admit that I'm not a dangerous guy, no hero blood flowing through these veins. But, while I was riding high and making the big bucks in college with my partner, karate and self-defense courses were the 'in' thing. I did earn a brown or black belt or something while hanging out with the serious jocks.

I raised my eyes as I crossed the threshold, finding myself looking right down the barrel of Bill's .38. Faith and the girls were sobbing in the corner booth. Bill was lying on the floor with Mae behind the counter, her hands raised. I moved into the room at the stranger's instruction, noticing Bill turn his head toward me.

Happy to see he was unharmed I looked back at the stranger. His eyes were on me, steel blue, cold, showing no emotion, "on the floor!" he ordered. I smiled at him and said, "did I over-cook your egg, I can do it again, no reason to get upset."

His eyes clouded as his mind struggled to interpret what I had said. While he was thinking I had moved a step closer to him without his notice, but Bill had. He shook his head, indicating that I should comply. I was within five feet of the gun barrel now, it pointed right at my nose, and yet I felt nothing. It was as if I were watching from a booth across the room. He had regained his mental capacity.

"Okay Bum, or whatever they call you, how'd you like to have one right between the eyes?"

I reasoned that he had simply reached over and lifted Bill's gun out of its holster, and before Bill could respond, he assumed control.

I continued to smile, taking a half step forward. "You could do that, but you'll have to take off the safety first," I said.

The moment he looked at the gun, I grabbed it and his hand, moving it up and aside, then pulled him toward me in a single motion. All of that practice in SoCal those many years ago came back to me. As he stumbled forward, I stepped aside and tripped him, still holding the hand and the gun tightly. As he hit the deck, a shot went off into the floor in front of him.

Buffy came running out, eyes as big as saucers. Bill was on his feet in an instant, having the man's arms pulled up behind him and cuffs being applied. Mae was shaking as I gathered her into my arms for a long moment and then turned my attention to Faith and the girls who had stopped crying and were staring at me.

All at once I felt shaky, weak, and exhausted myself as I sat down by them. "Ice cream anyone?" I asked, trying to regain my composure.

It seemed like several minutes before anyone spoke. Tina finally smiled, "could I have it in a cone to go?" she asked.

That brought down the house and put everyone back at ease. Bill was on his radio reporting to dispatch and asking if Tom was still in the area. Mae and Buff had sat down, and the stranger was in a chair in handcuffs.

"Sure darlin'," I answered Tina, "anyone else?" Both girls followed their little sister's lead as I moved to the freezer and began scooping cones. Before I was done, everyone in the room was licking ice cream and talking nervously at once, reliving the ordeal, except of course our ornery guest.

The rest of the day Saturday was anti-climactic, but not slow. As the community began to hear, they came by to relive the story with us over and over. Buffy became the official storyteller as I dipped ice cream until my arm ached and we finally ran out.

Tom and Bill left together to deliver their charge to the county jail but later returned to take our official statements for their reports. God was truly with us all. When asked why I suspected the man enough to take pictures, I said I just remember thinking why a big guy like that would only order so little, after taking a half hour to decide.

Tom surmised, and Bill agreed, that his plan to hold up the café had gone awry when law enforcement kept joining him at the counter for breakfast. He was in possession of a large knife but no gun until opportunity had provided itself. Tom took a call and repeated to the crowded room of guests that he was wanted in several states for armed robbery.

I was ready for a rest, but not well prepared to lead a church service when Sunday morning came. I envied God's trained servants, how easily it seemed that they would speak meaningful words and explain God's messages. I wished Jib were here this morning so that I could just sit back and absorb his considerable wisdom.

The usual congregation of faithful varied between a small handful to several dozen, depending on the season, the weather, or competing social events such as county fairs, harvest chores, or calving in the spring. For us at the Widespot, last week had been less demanding, therefore we had planned a potluck after service. My tired bones wished we had not.

Mae had all our carafes and coffee pots full of hot black coffee, hot water for tea bags, and a couple dozen 'store bought' donuts for the first comers. I had not had either time nor energy to do more than make a large potato salad and slice up a couple of donated water-melons before they began to arrive.

Jim Johnson, grocer, his wife and three children were the first in the door, each carrying their Bibles. Next was our friend Tom DeGrange, his wife and daughter, followed by Buck with wife and four sons. Whenever he attended I thought of Goliath. Faith and the three girls, Blake and his girlfriend, Al, the butcher, with Mary and their two granddaughters, and finally Bill Martin and his wife arrived to applause and good natured ribbing.

We also had several guests visiting various families and three who had stopped to eat but stayed for the service and the potluck. After several came in late, we had a head count of nearly forty, including children. I opened with prayer, giving God praise and thanks for His considerable blessings, then let the congregation add to my efforts. Several stood and recounted the blessings of the past week and their hope for the future before yielding the floor to another.

Blake surprisingly stood and thanked God for providing just the right person with whom to share his life and related to us that she had agreed to marry him after their graduation. As we prayed together, several acknowledged needs and asked for continuing prayer for God's help in their personal circumstances.

We are not much of a worship group the way big churches are, no band, piano, or worship leader. Interestingly, the only ones with a singing voice were one of Buck's sons, Thomas, and Faith Meyers. They however, were sufficient to help us through a couple of good old time hymns that everyone knew.

Finally it was time for my sermon. I had no plan, idea, or direction at all until I started speaking. It turned out that the sermon was about brotherly love, about Jesus' commandment to love one another as we love ourselves. I related the events of Friday concerning Mark and Becky and the two boys without specifically naming names of persons present, which would surely have embarrassed them. I just used the example that Buck and others had provided to support our need to think of others as more important that ourselves, giving God the credit for guiding us in the right direction. I was humbled when I realized He had provided the material for His own worship service.

We closed the service a shade before noon, with some returning home to get their food, while others to their car for theirs. Mae kept a fish bowl on the counter by the door that along with her tips included any tithe anyone wanted to leave. We used it to help those as needs presented themselves and for the annual printing of the church directory that was mailed to every home.

The "young bucks", as the 'old bucks' called them, never traveled anywhere without a football. They were outside throwing it around while the women were setting out the spread. Several wayfarers, ignoring the Closed sign, pulled into the parking lot for lunch. Some left, seeming embarrassed, two however stayed at the urging of the congregation and ate with us.

They were Betty and Ben, the brother and sister from Moscow who had gone to Athol to visit their grandmother Maggie Price. Her condition had worsened, the doctors diagnosing a bleed on her brain that was inoperable. She had slipped into a coma and would likely walk with the Lord very soon. The young couple were returning to the campus to wait for the grim news so they could return to bury her in her home town.

It seemed to me that being her last living relatives gave them responsibilities for which they had not yet been prepared. Mae took them aside and prayed with them, then offered to ride along when the time came that they might need help with the arrangements, saying that Maggie had been a good friend. She also packed them a basket of food to take on the road with them as they left.

In the manner of potlucks everywhere, there was an abundance of good food, each cook trying to showcase his or her specialty while trying unsuccessfully to remain humble amid the glowing compliments. When the day ended it was nearly four o' clock, the Widespot just locked its doors, each of us retiring to our private quarters, giving no thought to clean-up until morning.

Around 6:00, Buff knocked quietly on my door, "Bum," he said, "you awake?" I was and let him in. He had two fishing poles in one hand and a pail of worms in the other.

"I thought you might like to sit on the bank with me until dark and listen to the water," he said in almost poetic fashion. "I got an extra pole."

"I'd like that, Buff," I answered. "Listening to the water and maybe catchin' a fat trout might be just what I need."

As we walked through the lodge pole pines and scraggly cedars toward the meadow, I thought about Buff. I regretted that I had judged him by appearance, selling him way short. God had taken back some of his IQ but had replaced it with goodness and true wisdom. The little things he said made me feel humble when I considered their depth, like "listen to the water." How many wheelers and dealers took time to just listen to the water and let it caress their souls?

I felt comradeship and put my arm on his shoulder, "you are a good friend, Buff," I said. "Thanks for asking me to come along." He just smiled his 'full moon' smile without saying a word. I believe that God brings people into our lives for His own special reasons, sometimes to give us something we are lacking, other times for us to give of ourselves. I kind of think that is why I stopped by the Widespot the first time... they needed me and I them.

I wonder who first owned the café and what it was called then. Have you ever wondered what history a building or a place might hold, what dreams lived and died within the hearts of men as time and trials wore them down? Sometimes, when I get in a reflective mood like today, I wonder how it will all end. No, not the world, John the Revelator gave us that in the Revelation, but how it will all end for each of us before we walk in heaven with Jesus.

Will I, like Jib, stay here until I am called home? Will I find just the right woman, like Blake, and find I cannot live without her? Will we have children to carry forward our heritage? Or... will each day stand alone on it's own merits, the sum of them, the story of our lives? Sometimes, when prone to wax philosophical, I get bogged down in the unanswerable questions that plagued Solomon. He too found them impossible to answer.

Mae was looking her age today and maybe a bit more. The events of the last three days had taken their toll on all of us. I feared that the encounter with the robber had made her question her vulnerability and mortality. I decided to try and encourage her and give her a lift.

"Mae," I said, "have you ever tasted my banana cream pie?" knowing of course that she and no one in this world ever had.

"No," she said naively, "I didn't know you baked."

"Well," I said with confidence I did not feel, "you are about to. You are off the hook for dessert today." She gave me the smile I had hoped for, though a little drawn and halfhearted.

I had ordered a gallon of powdered vanilla custard, 2 gallons of whipping cream, an extra four dozen fresh eggs, and a major amount of ripe bananas in addition to my regular supplies. I knew that she would never let me buy pre-made pie crusts so I got out a recipe for what the author called 'easy-flaky pie crusts' and perused it while I did the prep for breakfast.

I cautioned her, "I cannot have you in my kitchen while I am cooking them. It's a secret, old family recipe." Buff listened, saying nothing as he overheard our conversation, but I could see him smiling as he filled and refilled the dishwasher with last night's dirty dishes.

I had gotten a good buy on link sausage from our supplier, so the morning special included them in every venue. Mondays were often slow, but not so this Monday. It was as if someone, somewhere, knew we were hitting on only three cylinders and was trying to test us. Sometimes it takes seconds to take an entire table's orders, other times ten minutes, with everyone wanting to inquire about and discuss every option.

Mae would just have turned in the order and someone at the table would change their mind. It didn't take long to remove the glow of the Sunday message from each of us. From time to time I looked up at Buff and seeing him smile in the midst of the turmoil helped me keep a firm hand on the tiller.

The breakfast rush was nearly over at 10:00 when I realized I had forgotten to pray this morning while prepping for the meal like I always did. I can honestly say I did not hesitate, but took my petitions right to the King while flipping flapjacks.

The lunch I had planned was a piece of cake for a cook under normal circumstances... sliced smoked turkey in a club sandwich with fries or open faced with mashed and veggies on the side. The turkey had been baked and sliced, all that remained was to serve it hot or cold, with fries or mashed potatoes and gravy. There were always a few who wanted a burger or dog that worked to break the rhythm, or Bill with his corned beef on rye, but overall, lunch was a ride in the park after suffering through breakfast. Praise God.

Tom stopped in for a milk shake on his way to join Bill at the arraignment for Robert Ahrens Sr., our robbery suspect and convicted felon. I bricked the grill and filtered the fryer grease, then turned to the business at hand, my pie crusts. The 'easy-flaky' recipe proved not as difficult as I had thought, soon I had 12 crusts in the oven browning. While they baked, I prepared the custard as per the label directions, adding a quarter cup of lemon juice and real Mexican vanilla in hopes to "make it mine."

I like to cook out of the box but using the box directions for a guide. As the custard cooled, so did the crusts on racks on every horizontal space I could find. Mae sidled by when she thought I was not looking and sampled a piece of crust, then smiled. It occurred to me that I wasn't fooling her a bit.

I began peeling and slicing bananas, stopping occasionally to place them on the floor of the cooled pie shells, on a whim I dusted them lightly with cinnamon before pouring the custard over them. As they skinned up I added another layer, sliced thinner this time, to the top, then set them on shelves in the walk-in.

Whipped cream was not the mystery to me that the other had been. When it began to peak, I added some of the pure Mexican vanilla and powdered sugar, then finished it up. I approved of the taste and set about smothering each pie liberally. When I turned my back, Mae grabbed a finger full of the whipped cream, getting caught in the process. She was looking less haggard now, regaining her easy smile and disposition, when she pronounced, "Good!"

I had seasoned two large prime rib roasts previously and now slid them into the already hot ovens to bake, while turning down the temp a hundred degrees. Then I wrapped and added several dozen bakers beside them. I made the base for the au jus from a commercial paste to which I would later add the good stuff from the roasts themselves. I had found you could never get enough to satisfy the customers from the roast beef alone.

Al's wife had given us several nice fresh horse-radish roots from her garden which I peeled and washed before blending them into a paste. Half I left for the purists who want it hot, the rest I blended with 'store-bought' into a sauce for the weak at heart.

Mae was sitting smiling at me when I finished. "You are God's own blessing, Bum, I know He sent you when He decided it was time to take Jib home." She had poured two cups of coffee and was waiting for me to join her. I was choking back tears just looking at her, so I changed the subject.

"How about a piece of pie with that coffee, just to make sure we don't poison our fancy clientele?"

She regained her composure and smiled, "sure, let me get it."

"No way," I replied, "my treat." I cut the pie in 8ths and we each took a saucer.

She tried to look surprised when she said, "not half bad... not bad at all." Although it was less than the best I had ever tasted it was good and the crust was flaky as promised.

The smaller of the primes was still rare when I took it out, knowing it would continue to cook, the larger was still only about 140º. The bakers came out and were placed as before in one part of the sink, butter was softened and ready to scoop, sour cream likewise. At 5:04 p.m. our first guests arrived, a family from Utah returning from Canada. They wanted fast and cheap with their five kids and a short budget. Burgers, fries, cokes, and onion rings filled the plates as Mae loaded the table and filled and refilled the soft drinks.

Faith and the girls were next, taking their usual booth. Faith asked for an end cut, petite and small burgers for the girls, catsup only, fries on the side. I did a big basket of fries, three baby burgers, pickles on the side, and a small cut of prime for Faith with baked spud and side salad.

Our friends Buck, wife, and the state champ front line came through the front door with grins. "Smelled somethin' burnin'," he said, "Bum cookin' again?"

I was tempted to stick out my tongue but restrained myself for fear of a beating. I grabbed the second prime out before it was ready just to make sure it was rare enough. I smiled as I sliced, "special is double burgers tonight, want cheese with that?" I asked.

"Yeah, six of them, rare with the good horseradish," he said as though I had never spoken.

As the place began to fill up I asked Buff for his help, knowing that Mae had her hands full out front. As the primes were plated, Buff split and filled the potatoes with scoops of sour cream and whipped butter, I added the au jus, bread, and horseradish, then sent them out the window. To add a little variety to the already overwhelming task at hand, there were a few who chose something off the menu, just enough to break our rhythm. To his credit, Buck became less vocal and demanding as the meal went on, possibly he or his wife could see our struggle to handle all our guests.

By 6:00 p.m. all of the entrees had been served and we were cutting and serving pie and coffee, having exhausted our supply of roast beef. Two carloads of travelers arrived late and were served from the grill while the tables were being bussed and dishes washed. We turned the sign around at 7:00 p.m., then settled at a table together sharing a single serving of prime I had set back and the remnants of a banana cream pie with our coffee.

We had served 40 dinners, cleaned up, and sat exhausted visiting and reliving the events of the last three hours. Mae smiled and put a crumpled napkin on the table, "Buck left us a tip" she said as she opened up my IOU that had replaced the usual $50 under his plate. Loud and demanding in some ways, yet humble and private in others, he had lived out Jesus' command to "love others as yourself."

"Mae", I said pausing to get her full attention, "I think we need to hire more help," and, I continued, "I think Buff here deserves a raise." I had caught her a little off guard, but could tell that she also had been aware that we were operating at full capacity and the business still growing daily.

"What do you have in mind?" she asked cautiously.

"You need at minimum a part-time to help you out front, and Buff is nearly able to run the kitchen himself now," I said.

Mae nodded agreement and then turned to Buffy, "we can add a hundred to your pay now and maybe more later if business continues to grow. Is that enough?"

Buff smiled and nodded enthusiastically, "that will be fine", he said. She looked back at me, "anyone in mind to help serve?"

I had been waiting for her to ask. "I've had an eye on Faith but I am unsure of how we could approach her without making it seem like asking her to earn what we are already giving her," I said.

Mae paused and then said, "She'd be a good choice alright if we can get around a couple of issues. It might be just the thing for her confidence and Lord knows she could use the money. She has shared that she may have a possible part time position at the library during the school year. What do you think Buffy?"

Buff seemed impressed that he had been given a voice on the subject. "Well, she sure is friendly, knows almost everyone, and needs to be around people more, I think," he observed.

"I agree Buff," I said, "it would be good for her to get out and be with adults some of the time rather than sitting at home and missing her husband all day long. It might help her heal."

Mae looked me right in the eye and said, "business is up right now, we do have the extra to make the changes, but what if it doesn't last?"

It was my turn to smile, "faith, my dear lady, it is our part to trust in God and do His will as we see it. He gives and takes away, we don't understand why, but we should know it is for our benefit always. We just have to play the hand He's dealt to us."

She smiled, "that is somethin' Jib would have said."

Don Taylor came in with a hand full of mail and an empty stomach. He was a light eater who usually ate at home and just had coffee at the Widespot when he made his rounds. Today, however, he asked for two over medium, wheat toast and links with his hash browns before joining Buff at the counter.

I turned the sign to Open just in time to welcome our recent friends Mark and Becky with their two sons. They had gotten an early start, leaving Moscow without eating and were ready to both visit and eat before they headed toward Canada.

"How's the new car working?" Buffy asked them between mouthfuls.

"Wonderful!" answered Becky, "we like it much better than the one we lost."

"Good mileage too!" Mark turned to Buff asking about fishing. Buff replied that he hadn't been since but still had their trout in the freezer for them. The boys were overjoyed.

"Do you have a ice chest?" Buffy asked. It turned out that their larger one had been ruined in the wreck but they had a new smaller one for drinks. I volunteered the disposable styrofoam one that I had just gotten from Al with the salmon, wrapping the fish first in old newspaper and then in a plastic bag before icing them down.

Out at the car, Mark thanked me again for our help and then asked for Buck's address so he could send them a note. Mae was visiting with Becky and the boys when we returned, Buff had placed their order on the flattop before getting back to his meal.

As I plated their orders, including the cartoon cakes, several regulars entered, seating themselves and filling their own cups. Mae got to her feet, greeted and took their orders as Faith and the girls entered. Mae winked at me and went to their table sitting beside Faith, not unnoticed by Buff who took them water and orange juice as per their usual. The girls liked to tease Buffy and did so relentlessly, giggling as they did. I was 'turnin' and burnin' as the sailors say, keeping up but not gaining as more joined us.

Mae cut their conversation short when I hit the bell for the second time and began to serve the waiting tables. Buff continued to bus tables and pour refills before heading toward the sink. We were an efficient and well-oiled machine once more. Tom entered, seated himself at the bar, ordered four scrambled and white toast dry, and a fruit cup. Taking a ribbing from the locals about the 'cup', he explained he was watching his cholesterol. That brought another round of laughter from those who pointed out the plate of eggs in front of him. A little after 10:00 a.m., Blake showed up with the week's meat order.

I re-congratulated him on his engagement as I paid his bill and offered him a bite to eat. He said he was running behind, but grabbed two links and a hot cake right off the grill, wrapped them up like a hot dog, gave me a grin and left out the back door. By the time the breakfast rush was over, the total in the till showed nearly $200, almost double what we had averaged on Mondays last year.

As I bricked the grill and cleaned up, I could see Mae again visiting with Faith who had stayed on after finishing her meal. I assumed she had found a way to make the job offer to her and they were discussing it now.

I had no special in mind for today's lunch so I just went with the menu, slicing some onions, racking the cheese, filling the pickle and lettuce bowls and starting my soup, before grabbing a stool at the counter to eat my eggs and toast. When Faith and the girls left, both Mae and Buff joined me.

"Well?" I said, waiting.

Mae answered, "Faith was hesitant at first, had never worked since high school, lacked the confidence she should have. But, she wants to give it a try, starting tomorrow. She still needs to work out the childcare arrangements long term. Short term they'll just stay here and hang out."

Buffy offered, "they're nice well-mannered girls, better than most." I nodded my agreement while amazed at his assessment of them.

A few minutes later Bill joined us, taking a stool at the counter. Mae handed him the menu as I slipped away to put his corned beef on rye together before dropping the rings into the hot grease. Bill looked up and smiled at me, "I think I'll try something different today," he said, then began to laugh.

"You should have seen the look on your face, Bum. I really gotcha didn't I?"

Even Mae was laughing as I turned over the sandwich and put his rings in a basket.

"Seriously now, Bum, I want to thank you for maybe saving our lives the other day when that Ahrens character got hold of my gun. I also want to warn you not to take the law into your own hands again," he said sternly.

"No need," I answered, "I have no plans to become Charles Bronson looking for wrongs to right. It scared me plumb to death after it was over."

Mae was smiling, "you're sounding just like Jib again. The few times I got him to talk about his bein' a hero and all, in the war, that was just what he said. Guess folks never plan to be a hero. It just comes to them when they need it." Both Bill and Buff were nodding agreement.

Bill blessed his food quietly and began to eat, then looked up at me with a smile.

"One of these days I'm gonna order breakfast or somethin' and you'll have to eat this yourself," he said. That got me to thinking about tomorrow's special, maybe corned beef and cabbage. I'd have to call Al and see if he had any available since I didn't have time to season and do my own brisket for tomorrow.

"Buff," I asked, "have you ever made corned beef and cabbage?"

He shook his head no, then smiled and said, "but I ate it."

I got Al on the phone. He had 15 lbs available all seasoned, aged, and ready to go so I asked him to hold them for me. About then the lunch crowd all came through the door at once. Mae seated twenty in about five minutes as Buff took them water and passed out menus.

Another dozen, including Buck and one of his sons, followed on their heels, filling up almost every seat except at the counter. As folks came and went Mae was able to keep up with Buffy's help, but I lagged behind filling orders in the order she brought them to the wheel. I made a mental note to visit with Mae about considering a lunch menu separate from the dinner one.

As it was, I had a table with three burgers waiting on a single of chicken fried steak and mashed potatoes with gravy. We'd been operating with the same menu since I joined Jib, when we were serving half the number of meals with two of us in the kitchen. The mad rush lasted for an hour and half and then they disappeared like summer snow.

I grabbed a big Gott cooler, iced it down and then threw it in the back of Jib's old pickup. Buff joined me as we drove down to Al's to get the corned beef.

"I knew her you know," Buff said right out of the blue. "Went to school with her when we was kids."

It caught me off guard, but also caught my interest, "who?" I asked.

"Faith," he answered as if I should have known all along.

"Oh, is that so?" I answered.

"Yeah, we started school together," he continued, "went all the way through until I crashed my bike. After that I was always a grade behind her. I hurt my head real bad, missed a lot of school, and even when I got better, it still takes me longer to understand things." Jib or Mae had told me some of the story but not the part about Faith.

"We were boyfriend-girlfriend up until I got hurt," he said natural like.

We got the meat, then headed back to the Widespot. As I drove, I was thinking about what he had said and it came to me that his interest in Faith and her girls may be more than casual. As we pulled up out behind I said, "you still like her like that Buff, boyfriend-girlfriend?"

At first he looked kind of alarmed, as though I had accused him of something bad, but calmed and answered, "it's different now, we're both older and she has the girls."

"You are right, my friend," I said. "But sometimes our feelings for someone don't change." We dropped the conversation and went inside and back to work.

I had put a nice boneless pork butt in the oven this morning on low heat, when I checked at 1:00 it still needed a bit more but now at 2:30 it was pull-apart tender. I took it out to cool, then checked my supply of flour tortillas, I had four dozen of the large ones left in the walk-in cooler. So all of a sudden it became Mexican night.

I had nearly ten pounds of shredded cheddar jack, sour cream, cilantro, and onions with several cans of refried beans on the shelf. The clock said 3:00 as the rice water came to a boil, I knew I was pushing it a little and so asked Buff to begin shredding the pork while I sliced, then chopped onions.

I turned the grill down and greased it lightly, waiting for the temp to drop a little while stirring the pot of refried beans. When Buff had finished, I began to throw the tortillas on the grill. When they softened, I turned them and placed them on a sheet pan. Buff began putting pork on them, adding the cheese, onions, beans and sour cream before rolling them up. I also sliced peppers but elected to serve them on the side. The burritos went back into the oven covered with foil at about 3:30 while we concentrated on the rice.

I know nothing about Mexican cooking but do like to eat and have eaten some of the best. I therefore was walking in faith and copying what I thought I had tasted. The freezer held two nice sacks of frozen whole kernel corn that I decided to use to supplement the rice. Kicking the grill back up, I oiled it with golden oil, then dumped a full bag of frozen corn on it along with chopped onions and colored bell peppers for looks. I left it all long enough to get a little scorched color, turning it often, then reduced it to a deep pan in the steam cabinet.

When I tasted it I added chili powder, salt, and pepper, then duplicated the process with the second bag. Buffy had drained the rice in a colander and was awaiting further instructions as the clock read 3:45. Together we added paprika, chili powder, and liquid chili sauce, looking more for the right color than taste. God blessed us, giving both. At 4:00 straight up, the white board displayed the special of the day as Mexican Fiesta $7.95.

Our first table of four ate the special with great relish, asking for corn chips, which I had forgotten until now. The two bags on hand proved to be insufficient for the night but sufficient enough to let God humble me a little. As the night wore on, several car loads of travelers joined the locals, leaving not a single burrito left over. At 6:00 I turned off the grill, not having taken a single order for anything fried off the menu. I did drop a couple of orders of French fries for kids but otherwise nothing. Buffy took a break during a slow period and ate a plate himself before copying Jib in saying "fit to eat."

Buck and family were absent but Tom and his wife and daughter, Bill and family, Al and his wife, Blake and his future bride, Faith and the girls, and our sometimes preacher and his wife from Priest River were among the four dozen served. Clean up was a snap with me having time to help bus tables and take money, Buff running the dishwasher full out, and Mae doing the dance among the tables.

When Mae closed out the till, the evening meal approached $500. I felt guilty and wondered if I should have charged less. Mae, however, was all smiles as she took a hundred off the top and put right in the tip jar with the Sunday offering.

I find it often very hard to try and determine from where our prosperity comes, while knowing of course it all comes from the Lord. What I mean is, why all of a sudden is this little wide spot in the road a haven to so many hungry folks? Interesting that just yesterday we had taken a leap of faith with Buffy and Faith and already God had chosen to bless our decision.

As I lay awake thinking in my cabin that night, I wondered how it all works. Does God wait on us to make a move, does He cause us to make a move, or did He already know that we would make that move and was there ready with the blessings for our choices? I drifted off to sleep happy, looking forward to Tuesday, eager to see what God might do at the Widespot.

PART THREE

"Bum!" "Bum!" Buffy yelled through the door, "wake up, we got trouble!"

I glanced at the clock while jumping up and into my Levis, it read just after 4:00 a.m. The sun was not up and yet as I walked outside the sky was red in the east. Buffy motioned to the front of the café where I could see both Tom's state car and Bill's county cruiser. They were both talking with a man I had never met before, standing beside a yellow commercial-looking fire rig with a Bureau of Land Management sign on the door.

"There's a big fire over to the east toward the county line," Buff said excitedly, "they say it's in the big timber, moving fast toward Buck's ranch. They already have planes and helicopters up from Boise dumping water on it, trying to slow it down, but the wind is blowing the wrong way."

I joined the men just as Mae walked up also asking, "what can we do to help?" The BLM man, Trent Davis took the lead, "we'd like to use the café as our base of operations if you are agreeable. How many acres do you have here?"

Mae answered, "a little over four if you count the land back by the cabins and the parking lot."

Trent laid out the hurriedly prepared plan, they wanted to use the Widespot to bivouac the firefighters, they'd need access to showers and a place to set up a big tent as a mess hall, as well as an area for sleeping tents. He offered to contract with us for three meals a day plus extra for expenses like additional labor and consumables like soap, toilet paper, and the like. We were still hammering out details when Glen Gardner, a local farmer, came forward and interrupted us.

He introduced himself to Davis and offered an idea. "I'm a crop farmer, I've known Buck since high school and I may have an idea that could save his ranch."

"Go ahead," Davis said, although there was an element of urgency in his voice.

"Buck has a pond on his property, uses it to flood irrigate his pasture land, maybe five or six acres across but I have no idea how deep."

"Yes," Davis agreed, having already seen the pond and made plans to use it, "I am aware of it, we estimate it at 300-400,000 gallons."

"I could have my wheel line set up on his pasture near the timber and ready to pump water in less than a day with some help."

Davis warmed to the idea, "the heat from the fire would turn his green pasture into tinder in less than an hour," he informed us. "Your sprinklers would not only cool the grass but also hydrate it at the same time, providing us time to fight it. How far away is the equipment?" he asked.

"It's already loaded and on it's way," Glen said, "but I thought I'd best stop and get the nod before I jumped in. I already have about ten volunteers headed out there with their gear."

For the first time Davis smiled, "we might have a chance yet," he said. "Let me know what you need and I'll make sure you have it." He handed Glen a mobile phone as he did.

"Generator, we'll need a sizable generator to operate my pump and won't have time to string a line," Glen answered, "and fuel for it."

"Done," said the BLM chief, "consider it there."

Glen left at a trot for his pickup with two following. Davis was already on the phone arranging air delivery, giving the coordinates of Buck's pond and Glen's name as the go-to guy. We could hear, but not clearly see, the firefighting bombers flying overhead in the pending sunrise, dumping their loads of fire retardant on the fire.

Men and equipment began to arrive, first a trickle, then a steady stream. It appeared to me that most were support crew and not the actual firefighters, setting up tents and equipment much like that of a military operation preparing for a prolonged conflict.

Inside the Widespot, Mae was on the phone calling names, first of local church members, and then her personal friends. She was asking each in turn to call others, thus spreading the word north and south along the corridor for fifty miles. I was intrigued and amazed by her efficiency and analytical approach to the emergency.

Several she hired for an indeterminate period to help make and pack lunches. She also arranged to use the vacant church as a day care for the new hires, finding several willing to staff it. Including Faith, Buffy, and myself we now numbered twenty-four.

We sat down and worked out schedules for three eight-hour shifts with Mae taking the first, me the second, and Buffy the third. Then we began calling our teams and scheduling their arrival times. When we finished, I awoke Al and ordered all of the frozen burger patties he could get his hands on, ditto sausage, and ham. Next, I called our milk supplier who was already at work and ordered bulk as well as individual cartons.

They were able to also hook me up with a bottled water supplier who promised 100 cases by noon. Our little walk-in cooler was quickly rearranged in preparation for the on-slaught of expected deliveries. I knew, however, that we had insufficient freezer space, so I called Al back and arranged to rent his old freezer truck for the over-flow. He jumped at the idea of it making money rather than sitting unused behind his business. It also made it easier for him to load and deliver without having to unload.

Buffy and Mae were still calling their crews and discussing details as I left to find Trent Davis. My question to the man was how many, for how long? He covered the phone on which he had been speaking, shook his head, then smiled grimly, "figure 100-150 initially, two weeks at a minimum."

Then he followed it up with, "could be double or triple that if we don't get a break in the weather." I turned to walk away as he hung up the phone.

"Quite a community you have here," he commented. "I've never seen anything like it. That Glen Gardner, he's quite a man. I wish I had someone like him on my team all the time." I nodded, smiled, and returned to join the help assembling inside the café.

In the kitchen I counted my resources, then made a quick call to the commissary who provided many of our staples; sliced meats, lettuce, butter, bread, cheese, and condiments, both bulk and individual servings. I reminded myself to contact my broker and access some funds first chance I got, knowing that the reimbursement from the government would come slowly and that we'd need working capital to pay the locals in a timely manner.

Buffy's crew showed up first, including Faith. I let him take charge, amazed at his orderly approach to things. They pushed several fours together, covered them with clean table cloths and began assembling the ingredients necessary for sandwiches. We had only ten commercial loaves on hand, enough for roughly eighty sandwiches, until our order arrived.

We did, however, have plenty of sliced cheddar and three pre-cooked hams that I ran through the slicer for Buff and his crew. With one case of lettuce and two of tomatoes, they were soon assembling and wrapping sandwiches. I called the commissary back and added 10 cases of assorted chips, packaged trail mix, and also energy bars at the suggestion of the person on the phone. As one can imagine, this was new to all of us, both in volume and scope.

Outside, they already had the would-be mess tent nearly up with a crew unloading folding tables like they had done this before. A second box van was filled with several hundred folding chairs. I approached Trent Davis again as he was shouting orders to each crew leader.

"Trent, this is new to us, do you have any kind of a list of things printed out? I keep "another-thinging" our suppliers until I am afraid they may hang up on me."

He took a minute to laugh, "I don't expect they will when they start ringing up the sales, but I do know what you mean. I'll have someone get you a list for a place to start. By the way, do you need front-money? I have a government charge card you can use if you promise to save the receipts." I accepted it gratefully, knowing that it would make our financial lives much easier.

When I returned inside, the phone was ringing, with no one taking notice. I picked it up and found it was the commissary calling us back. Some resourceful salesman was on the phone wondering why I had ordered no consumables like paper plates, forks, napkins, and paper sacks. I thanked him for his concern and followed his lead before giving him the credit card information to cover both orders.

Mae reappeared just as I had hung up, "how's it going?" she asked.

I filled her in as I watched Buff and his crew working efficiently and happily together. It was after daylight when our first suppliers began to arrive and the smoke from the fire began to fill the canyon.

The gravel turnout across the highway from the café became the landing spot for the helicopter, dropping in men and their personal supplies. The first time I saw the smoke jumpers I was reminded of a wolf, they had a hungry look about them, as though they were hungry for the adventure and the danger the fire posed to them.

Like a wolf, they seemed of a size... lean, durable, and fearless. Another thought that came to mind as I watched them was of young knights heading fearlessly to the crusades, eager to do battle for a cause. The actual jumpers numbered only a couple dozen, maybe less, but the support teams and tanker teams had grown to nearly a hundred.

I was following the progression with interest when Mae reminded me I should be resting to be ready for the 12:00-8:00 p.m. shift. Outside, Al had pulled his freezer truck alongside the building at the rear while Blake was unloading a second truck into our walk-in cooler. By the time he had filled our orders, we were bursting at the seams with perishable merchandise. He readily accepted the government charge card, then asked if I thought he should inventory more at his own business. I was cautious about committing to more than we could use, so I told him to give us a couple of days to get a handle on things. I promised to let him know as things developed.

Trent must have seen me and came trotting over, eager to share what little news he had. "Glen and the crew have the wheel lines operational already, did a test run and it works just like he had hoped. Buck has moved his herd west away from immediate danger but plans to stay and fight, they have no plans to leave. How are the provisions coming?"

"We have about thirty including Buck and his family out there who will need lunch in a couple of hours. Buff and his team should have about eighty meals ready soon", I said. "Would you look them over and give us an idea if they are adequate?"

Trent smiled, "Sure, I'll eat one myself. It's been a long morning."

I went inside and began cooking, mostly for the help and then a few from the crew outside joined them. Buff and his group enjoyed burgers, fries, and soft drinks as a perk of the job, taking a breather from their labors. I made special note that he and Faith sat next to each other, visiting as they ate. When Trent came in, having smelled the food, he deferred from the sack lunch and ordered off the menu, as did his crew. The few regulars who showed up at lunch time did so mostly out of curiosity, asking questions, eating and leaving.

The commissary delivery showed up just in the nick of time to provide bottled water to go with the sack lunches as a crew delivered them to Buck's ranch. I had not had time to notice Mae had been gone until she rejoined us with a glass of iced tea in her hand. She had been making room in one of the vacant cabins to use as storage for our extra paper products, toiletries, and dry foods like bread and chips.

At Trent's suggestion, we added fresh fruit to our lunch sacks, I added both oranges and apples to the order I was already compiling for tomorrow.

"We'll be dropping a dozen jumpers in within the hour" he confided to us. "All they have is what they are able to carry." Of course that made sense and maybe explained the hungry wolfish look they had.

"Trent," I said in a minute of generosity, "if you'll ask them in, I'll fill them up with good lean protein."

"While he was outside relaying my invitation, I cut both back straps out of a whole beef and began to butterfly them. Beer batter, home fries, and fresh cut onion rings made me feel like I was part of the "war effort".

If not for their lean appearances I'd have sworn they were Buck's family, eating every bite, then looking around to make sure they missed nothing. They turned down our offers for soft drinks or milk shakes however, choosing to drink only water. Although they did not pay for their meal, each of them left Mae a tip under their water glass as they filed out. I said a silent prayer for them, feeling much as I would have for soldiers going off to war. I boiled three pots of potatoes, 50 lbs total, somewhat undecided whether to mash or shred them for hash browns. Then put another 50 lbs in the ovens to bake.

I could see that I was over my head in organizing an ongoing menu consistently for a hundred plus people for an indeterminate period.

Buff joined me and without conversation began washing and chopping fresh carrots until he had a 5 gallon pan full, covered in water. He showed one of his crew how to operate the dishwasher and set him about scraping plates and washing dishes. Faith, Mae, and the rest of the crew were wrapping silverware and plastic ware in napkins for later use. I cleaned out the ice-maker, filling four plastic buckets which went out into Al's freezer as backup while fresh was being made.

"What do ya' think, Buff, coleslaw?"

Buff nodded, "yup, everyone likes good coleslaw and it's good for you."

"And, I was thinking, it's quick and easy too," as a half dozen heads of cabbage gave their lives for the cause.

With both ovens full of potatoes, I didn't have room for the roasts I had prepared, so I filled the barbecue with charcoal, then prepared to roast them. Using a temperature of 125 and then figuring a minimum serving of lean meat at 6 ounces, adding 15% for waste and shrinkage, I put a total of 54 lbs of roast beef over the charcoal fire. More than I had ever cooked before in my life. I had a note pad in my pocket with which to later verify or correct the validity of my calculations.

"Mae," I asked when I returned inside, "did Jib ever hire any local help?"

"The only time we ever left was once when he took me to Hawaii on our anniversary," she answered. "He hired Matt Dexter from Hayden Lake who used to own a restaurant."

"How did he do?" I asked.

"Well, Jib said, he 'never burned it down' when I asked him the same question. Guess he must have done alright. Why you askin', think we need more help?"

"I do," I admitted. "We have three shifts, and three shift leaders, but only two cooks. It wouldn't be fair to expect you to cook and serve too."

She closed her eyes a moment, possibly asking God for direction, then answered, "let me give Matt a call and see what he's doin' now."

Back in the kitchen, Buff was peeling and chopping onions, his head down with tears running down both cheeks. He was doing his best to help get me ready for my shift in four hours. I made note that I needed to do the same for my own relief in twelve.

Our situation made it necessary to plan two meals ahead. In the future Buff would have the first shift, 4 a.m. to 12 p.m., probably the breakfast shift for many. I'd have the lunch/dinner, 12 p.m. to 8 p.m.

shift and Mae and possibly Matt would handle the night from 8 p.m. to 4 a.m. So here was Buff, helping me prep for dinner, then I'd begin to prepare whatever Mae determined she wanted on hand, then she'd hand the ball off to Buff again.

I was beginning to get it worked out in my head but wanted Trent and the crews' input about what to expect during the night. Trent rejoined us for a few minutes while I laid out my thoughts to the group.

"How do we plan for the night shift?" I asked.

Trent smiled, "just like the day, when they get in tired and hungry they don't care if it is 4 a.m. or 4 p.m., so breakfast can be meatballs or scrambled eggs, either way."

That made my thought process re-calibrate, but it made the planning much easier. "Mae," I said, "let's close to the public or at least not let them order off the menu and focus our attention on the firefighters and their needs."

She nodded in agreement, "we can't be everything to everyone 24/7." We did a little toast and Trent went back outside to work.

Spaghetti. I fired up 25 lbs of ground beef and made a meat sauce which Mae could heat and serve any time with the pasta. Things were beginning to fall into place until twenty-five hungry men came in looking for food while the thermometer still showed 140º on the roasts. I custom cooked 25 chicken fried steaks, grabbing some of the bakers out of the oven before boiling Buff's carrots. Buff smiled and kept chopping, finishing up where I had left off on the cabbage.

I tried to imagine how military cooks operated and planned to do the same. As the thermometer neared 160º I pulled all of the roast beef off the grill and placed them in portable roasters on low heat. I began slabbing them about a half inch thick, which our old scales said averaged about seven ounces before returning them to the roasters, swimming in au jus. While Buff whipped up several gallons of packaged gravy, I turned the ovens off, leaving the bakers inside to stay hot.

Trent's lead man stuck his head in the kitchen, "okay to send in more?" he asked.

"How many?" I asked. "We can seat and feed about forty-five comfortably inside, easier for us and more comfortable for them, any more and we gotta take it out to the tent."

He smiled, "we'll send in forty-five at a time then."

"Buff, your crew ready to feed?" I asked, watching he and Faith smile at each other. We began plating the roast beef, freshly mashed boiled potatoes with gravy, carrots, bakery rolls with butter, as each of our new servers began to set out drinks and deliver the meals. I thanked God for allowing us time to prepare.

Mae had gone to bed, having been up most of the night and day.

My crew had arrived and was taking instruction from their peers who were ready to go home to their families. As they left, I asked that they leave their names, SS#'s, and home phone numbers on a pad Mae had left by the register. I told them they would receive a full day's pay for their short service and thanked them for their help.

My crew, who would work until midnight, included many that I knew well as customers or from church on Sundays. I walked out front for a moment, immediately tasting the unpleasant smell of the approaching fire and feeling the heaviness in the air.

I looked, anticipating a crowd of forty five gathered waiting to be fed, but only saw about ten tired hungry men sitting on the ground waiting their turns.

"Come with me guys," I said, motioning toward the café, "I can find another ten chairs and some hot food for you." They looked toward the lead, who smiled and motioned them to follow me inside. I have previously mentioned the 'over flow' area that we used sometimes for bazaar sales in the winter. It took only a few minutes to rearrange it and free up three additional tables. Myrna, who I remembered had a particularly nice singing voice at church, took the lead among the servers, setting out silverware and drinks, then the roast beef platters as I prepared them.

Trent himself and a few stragglers joined us as we cleaned up from the first bunch, enjoying their dinner. One of my crew was a young man, maybe twenty, needing the work. I educated him on the workings of the dishwasher and showed him around the kitchen.

After the tables were bussed, the women began preparing the glasses, cups, and silver services for the next shift. I showed them where to find the condiments to fill the containers and the sugar and creams. As there was a break in the activity, I asked them to sign the sheet with their names and personal info right below the first shift. Someone asked if I needed help in the kitchen, they having a friend with experience. I made no promises but encouraged them to call.

With nearly enough roast beef to feed another meal, I prepared to have baked spaghetti ready as Mae might need it. Twelve pounds of spaghetti noodles boiled for 10 minutes then drained, with olive oil to keep it from clumping, went into two 4½ gallon portable roasting pans, mixed thoroughly with the marinara meat sauce I had prepared earlier. I covered the mixture with a thick layer of grated Parmesan cheese and chopped parsley and then aluminum foil before sitting them inside the cooler.

I had six loaves of French bread sliced lengthwise which I covered with ground garlic butter and more parsley flakes, then foiled, to go into the oven when needed. About 8:00 another group of tired hungry workers joined us for a meal.

Afterward, we began the process of making sandwiches for the lunches from our supply of sliced meats from the commissary. By 11:00 we were all tired to the bone, not having adjusted to the routine or our sleep patterns. Mae and her crew showed up a little before midnight, with sleepy eyes, but with determination and the will to carry on. I showed her what remained of the roast beef and mashed potatoes, the baked potatoes, and the sack lunches ready to send out.

Both pans of spaghetti were waiting to be baked, then served with the garlic loaves. As we said goodbye and left to catch a few hours of sleep, Trent came in with a report on the fire. The wind was still push-ing it westward toward the ranch but had been slowed by the retardant drops and the lower nighttime temperatures. It was more than ten miles east of Buck's property and moving more slowly. We each said our own prayers of thanks and petition before leaving.

I slept soundly until nearly 8:00 a.m., surprised to have not been awakened at my normal 6:00, showered, dressed and walked to the Widespot where Buff and crew were relieving Mae and her cohorts.

The smoke jumpers had been picked up and were looking dirty and tired when I entered, eating quietly and purposefully. I grabbed the OJ pitcher and began filling glasses as Faith and her crew refilled coffees and bussed tables. Buffy seemed to have everything well under control in the back, with bacon and ham being fried ahead. He had several dozen slices of French toast in the warmer also, some of which became my own breakfast, others went to tables as seconds or thirds.

Buff smiled at me but said nothing, focusing on the job at hand. I elected to let him run his shift and not usurp his authority by jumping right in, saying only that I was here if he needed me. He nodded and thanked me as he finished up at the grill before joining me at the counter. "Mae used up the roast beef and mashed from last night and one pan of the spaghetti," he announced, "a big group had come in about 2:00."

"What have you got in mind?" I asked him. "Got any thought on what to cook yet?"

He smiled like he appreciated my comment, "how do Coney dogs and French fries sound?" he answered. "I just started the water heating, thought maybe I'd boil them rather than fry and they'd cook faster and hold longer."

"How many pounds of foot longs did Al send?" I asked.

"It looks like two 10 lbs which should feed about forty at two each," he said, having already done the math.

"Great idea," I said sincerely. "Where can I help?"

Buff smiled, "you could chop onions, I had my fill of that yesterday while I fry up some burgers and make the sauce."

I was interested in how he would make the sauce since we had never served it here, but said nothing.

"You got it buddy," I said, rising and heading back toward the walk-in to get the onions. I was chopping and trying to remember not to breathe through my nose while he broke down the bulk hamburger on the grill. His guy was humming and working behind us at the dish-washer and the girls were rolling silver and bussing tables as the jumpers headed toward the front door.

I caught up with them knowing that only three cabins were available for them to shower. I tossed my set of keys to the one in the lead, "mine is the one on the end, far left, soap and towels in the bathroom, lock it up when you're done." They smiled and said thanks as they headed to the showers and then bed.

About 10:00 Trent and several came in, finishing up the leftover French toast and bacon. "I am headed out to Buck's place," he said jovially to me, "want to tag along?"

I looked at Buff who nodded. "Under control," he said. We grabbed two boxes of sack lunches and a couple of cases of water and then headed out.

Interestingly, I had never strayed far from the Widespot. Having no vehicle of my own, I had ridden a few times with Jib or made runs to pick up supplies, but had never seen much of the valley. We traveled first south on state Highway 95, then turned east on a paved side road that soon became gravel as we approached the mountains. Buck had a high, wide gate at the entrance to his property, in the manner of most ranchers.

The size and construction of the gate bragged of their degree of success, as did the size of their barns. Often the house was average or less, but the barn was a showplace, an ego thing no doubt. The smoke filled the sky to the east from horizon to horizon, the red glow reflecting off the clouds spoke to its size and nature. Meg, I think Buck's wife's name was Meg. We had never been introduced and I had always thought of her as Mrs. Buck, rose from her station on the front porch.

Greeting us with a smile and genuine hospitality, she said my name reverently, 'Bum Roberts'. "Never thought I'd see you out of the kitchen." She stuck out her hand to Trent and introduced herself as Megan Spellman, or Meg to friends.

"Buck and the boys are out making sure the cattle had water and had been moved to the proper pasture," she advised us. She motioned toward the distant treeline at the end of the field, maybe a quarter of a mile from the house, where men were gathered at the pond. Behind them was a dense stand of trees that covered a massive hillside rising to disappear into the smoke and haze of the fire behind.

"Doesn't seem to be getting closer than it was last night," she observed in a matter of fact tone, "but it's hard to tell distance from here."

Trent replied, "the air tanker crews have slowed the westerly progress with retardant, but it is far from contained. We are hoping to get a perimeter to the north if the weather cooperates. She smiled sadly. "Such a waste," she said, "all of those years to grow and then gone in a few hours. Nature's way, I guess, but we don't have to like it." I immediately liked her and her common sense approach to life.

Trent interrupted our daydreaming, "well, I suppose there are men down there who might like a bite to eat," he said, pointing to the provisions we'd brought with us.

"'Spect so," she agreed, "I've got a chocolate cake baked, maybe you'd take it with you and save me the trip."

The men were pleased to see us and more than pleased to see the cake. Glen Gardner, his son and two others from the valley were there to man the pump and wheel line, about twenty others were there sporting firefighting gear, apparently forest service or BLM. We left the lunches and water, and gave them what sparse information was available. They, being too close to the mountain to have any line of sight to the fire, relied upon their phones for direction. They were encouraged by the news we did have.

Ten miles was just seconds by air, as we heard the bombers fly over to disappear into the tree line before dumping their precious cargo. As we were leaving, a helo with a bucket full of water hanging under it on a long tether passed over us, being directed to the most critical dump spot.

The air was still and thick, without wind the taste of ash and sulfur hung in the air, filling our noses and making our eyes water. Trent was on his phone while his notepad gave him an eagle's eye view of the fire from the vantage point of an air crew overhead. "Try and cut it off from moving north," I heard him say.

I could picture them making the stand to the west to save ranches and property, and to the north to prevent it following the ridge line to the more inaccessible high country. To the south, God had placed natural barriers in the form of many small lakes that were even now providing water to the water buckets hauled in by air.

As we neared the Widespot, Trent spoke. "We seem to be holding at about 50,000," meaning 50,000 acres I supposed without asking. At the Widespot I got my first overview of the command center. It looked like what I supposed might be a military encampment. The large, to this point hardly used command tent and mess hall, a single fire truck, a converted school bus for personnel transportation, two water carriers, a half dozen pickups and SUV's, and out back three or four dozen smaller tents scattered around the cabins. I supposed that coordinating it was akin to a military exercise. I looked at Trent with renewed respect.

Just as we got out, the twenty jumpers from last night exited the café, walking toward Trent. "We are going to try and get a perimeter on it to the north, we'll be dropping you on S-10" he said pointing to the map he held in his hand, S-10 indicating a particular mountain. The men nodded and then moved toward their gear in the staging area, their leader using the hood of the truck to spread his map. While they talked, pointing regularly to the map, I went inside to add my skills to the effort.

The next three days were carbon copies, with the crews coming and going, food being cooked and served, supplies waxing and waning as deliveries came. It became natural, almost mundane, taking on a routine as we fell into step with the events which determined our lives. Our 'new hires' became more and more efficient, less dependent upon instruction, and more involved in the war we waged, several however quit coming, choosing a life less demanding. While I tried to stay creative, and Buff as well, we soon ran out of ideas for practical menus, certain things being impractical to try and keep hot and fresh.

For their part, the fire crews never complained, often giving compliments or leaving tips, but never a criticism. That made it easy for us to want to work harder to do our part even better. Twice, since the ordeal had begun, Mae called and had our septic system pumped as it became overburdened. Once we had to have the big propane tank out back refilled, but overall, things went smoothly.

Saturday of the first week, we awoke to wind and rain, a mixed blessing. Trent mentioned the possibility of lightning strikes, but none caused additional fires in our immediate area. The rain settled the dust, took some of the crud out of the air, and gave everyone a short lived sense of cleansing. The wind, however, continued to blow after the rain stopped, soon revitalizing the fire and encouraging it to move westward once again, toward Buck's ranch.

It was actually Buffy who came to me with Faith's idea as I came on shift Saturday. "Let's hold a church service in the mess tent tomorrow, for both the locals and the firefighters." At first all I could see were roadblocks and reasons not to make our tenuous situation worse. Then a whisper in my ear encouraged me asking... Who rules the wind, the fire, the rain? The answer was self-evident. Our need for communion was all the more necessary because of our circumstance.

When I approached Trent with the idea, he embraced it with enthusiasm, much to my surprise, offering to include any extra meals in his own budget. I ran it past Mae who helped spread the word. Promising to stay past her shift to help Buff, I also planned to come in early to help as well.

Many of Mae's tired crew were joined by their families first for breakfast, then for worship, Buff's crew had invited family as well, and many of mine joined us. We made breakfast simple with hash browns, scrambled eggs, fried ham and toast self-served from a steam cabinet onto paper plates. The tent had room for over a hundred and was nearly filled with firefighters and locals when I arrived. Others came and went as necessary after eating, and during the service.

It was a little overwhelming at first, the whole scene, having the feel of a revival I suppose because of the tent. We sang along with a boom-box someone had brought as a local station played Christian music. I stood, not having any plan, and then began by recounting the story of my own unbelief just a day earlier.

"I suppose", I said, "we each when feeling overwhelmed with life, have a tendency to turn away rather than toward God. That is exactly what the Deceiver hopes and encourages us to do. He hopes we will try and handle life in our own strength, ignoring the only One who has the power to take away our troubles."

"Today we are here worshiping God, many feeling an urgency to resume the battle, thinking that this is time we might better spend fighting the fire. I am here to tell you today that our foe is not the fire, our foe is our unwillingness to trust in God's power, our pride, our lack of faith. Let's pray together now for God's will to be done, trusting in His promise that He desires good for those who believe in Him."

We prayed together for more than ten minutes, most quietly, some aloud, others leading prayers of their own with people joining in. I closed the short service, then someone hit the boom box for a final hymn. I don't remember feeling closer to God then that day, with both firefighters and locals embracing and hugging each other in the joy of the moment. Outside it had begun to rain again, the wind picking up.

It was almost like the mingling of generations at a family reunion when the remnants of the three crews dispersed after the service, we were three, but yet we were one. Buffy's shift was on duty and went back to work, doing prep work for my group who would take over at 4:00, while still feeding a few stragglers who had come from the fire lines. While it was still warm outside, the damp air gave us a feeling of the impending fall, still nearly a month away. Beef stew seemed appropriate for the evening meal.

Buff agreed with my idea and offered assistance as I began to break down one of the carcasses hanging in the cooler, first into roasts, then into lean bite-sized chunks. I heavily seasoned them, dredged them in flour and then browned them on the now vacant grill before sitting them aside and seasoning them once more as they cooled.

Both Buff and I busied ourselves with prepping carrots, onions, potatoes, and celery as I began to boil the bones, fat, and trimmings to make a broth. When I finished at the grill, Buffy began to fry hamburger for sloppy-Joes for his lunch crowd, his crew bagging lunches and wrapping napkins around forks to go with it.

As I finished my prep, Trent entered with a smile and an excited look on his face. "Wind is blowin' west to east," he marveled, "pushing the fire back on itself, the rain is helping too," he said.

"Thank God," I said aloud.

Trent went on, "it's a miracle. I've never seen anything like it before."

"Indeed it is", I agreed, "and you probably have but have not realized it before. Too many times we think we've caught a break, or had good luck, or something... never being willing to recognize when God answers our prayers or give Him the praise for it."

He gave me an odd look then said, "you know, you are right."

"I have always believed there is a God, but never considered much about Him being involved in our daily lives until now. Glad to say, my friend, that is how it usually begins for us... first we acknowledge His existence, then His power, then we experience His love, and finally we believe and accept salvation in Jesus."

I could tell he was trying to absorb it all, so I backed off, simply saying, "listen to your heart, it is trying to tell you something. You and I can talk any time." He left and I shared his good news with all those on duty before grabbing up the phone to call Buck and Meg. Meg laughed as she picked up the phone saying, "no Buck is not here, he's out dancing in the rain with the boys."

The rain continued into the afternoon before it stopped, leaving the clouds behind to block the sun. Local radio said we got nearly a quarter of an inch in the valley, more up in the mountains. At 4:00 my crew took over from Buff, everyone in a good mood and looking forward to their shift. As they left I noticed that Buffy had his arm around Faith. Some fires when lit, take longer to burn than others, I thought to myself.

I put the beef in the broth, having first taken out the bones, giving them time to boil before adding the vegetables which cook faster. Later on I would add the less durable veggies like broccoli and frozen corn just prior to preparing to serve. The bread man dumped off a bunch of brown and serve rolls that I readied to put into the ovens later and several dozen large hamburger buns for the sloppy Joes that Buff had planned.

As the men filed in and took their seats, our crew brought them drinks and visited openly asking about the progress being made in the fire. To a man, they seemed encouraged and enlivened, speaking for the first time of getting it under control. Both fryers were cooking to capacity as the home fries were cooked and then plated with Buff's sloppy-Joes and sides of his coleslaw.

Thinking far ahead, I took out the salmon heads, bones, and leftovers from our freezer in preparation to making some stock for fish stew, then picked up the phone and called Al, not thinking about it being Sunday. When no one answered, I left a message concerning our needs and asked for a call back. I had never made fish stew, only eaten it, but had a general idea of what I wanted to create.

For the first time since the fire, Buck came through the front door, this time alone and smiling. "Looks like God parted the Red Sea again for us," he chuckled. "You folks must have done a passel of prayin'" he added.

"That we did, that we did," I said as I came out of the kitchen to greet him. Rather than his usual smothering handshake, he hugged me like a big friendly bear. "Got any food?" he asked mischievously.

"What sounds good to you Buck," I asked.

"How about corned beef on rye with onion rings," he said. "I imagine with Bill busy you have missed cooking for him." This time we both laughed.

"Or," he continued, "maybe a little bit of that stringy steak Al has been sending you."

I smiled and cut off a nice piece of New York strip, hit it with garlic salt, pepper, and table salt, then threw it on the grill. I looked around and finally found a couple of left-over baked potatoes and plated a nice portion of Buff's coleslaw on the side.

As he sat at the counter watching he spoke again, "you know Glen Gardner and I were close friends in high school." I nodded. "Right up until we both started dating Megan," he said remembering the days.

"Even after both of us married, we didn't keep truck with each other much, still holding it between us." I nodded again, not knowing how to reply.

"We used to be best of friends, played ball together, it's a shame for all of those years we wasted. Glen really came through for us when we needed it most."

Finally, I got a voice and said, "have you told him?"

"Don't know how," Buck answered, "so much water run under the bridge, I am embarrassed." I brought his plate to him with a full pitcher of milk and then joined him at the counter. He was quiet for a moment, blessing the food I supposed, and then began to eat with a troubled look still on his face.

"How about just like you told me," I said, "lay it all out plain and easy, right in front of him. Let God do the rest. There's a verse that talks about that, something about not offering up your sacrifice before you make amends with a friend."

He smiled, "I know the one," he said nodding his great bald head.

My crew was busy dipping the sloppy-Joe meat onto the buns and then wrapping them in foil before nesting them in the roasting pans to stay warm. "How many still out at your place?" I asked Buck.

"About 25 including Meg and the boys," he answered, "but you don't have to send anything down to them, I've got the best part of a prime rib already on the Traeger, would take a gallon or two of that coleslaw though."

I smiled, reminding myself I needed to tell Buffy that his coleslaw was a big hit. He left with a gallon jug under each arm, but not before leaving $50 in Mae's fish bowl beside the register. My crew used up the last of the coleslaw, placing it in to-go's with lids, then into the cooler until the need presented itself. I began water for potatoes, with potato salad in mind for later on, then took a break over an iced tea.

Our stew was ready and simmering when the first of the fire fighters came through the doors about five. Rolls were heating in the oven when I added pasta to the mix to give it more body. Within a few minutes the bowls were finding homes, the rolls served 'family style' in the middle of each table with butter and fresh jam. Our crew scurried to bring condiments as each man seasoned his own to taste.

These men brought with them a look, like the last, of hopefulness rather than worry, laughing and joking aloud as they ate most of my first five gallons of stew. More rolls went into the oven to warm while I added pasta to the second pot of stew. Chairs emptied and refilled until about 6:00 when Trent and his lead men joined the last of them.

Our crew had moved to the "overflow" area to begin filling the sacks for the crew still in the field, including the jumpers who were still on the mountain. Trent moved to the counter. I continued to work on five gallons of potatoes, boiled eggs, chopped pickles and onions, assembling them into something resembling a salad, as he began to speak.

"You seem to know about what I'm feeling" he said quietly, possibly to keep from being overheard. I stopped cooking and joined him at the counter.

"Maybe. Maybe I do," I said in response. It took several minutes to give my witness, speaking slowly and carefully, remembering the event clearly as I shared. I watched as he nodded several times affirming his understanding and agreement.

"How did you come to the point?" he asked.

"Well," I said... "I think Jesus had been knocking on the door of my heart for some time. I had ignored Him. Jib, Mae's husband, just helped me answer the door when the time was right. Are you thinking that the time may be right for you?"

He nodded, tears already forming in his eyes, "yes... yes, I think so." I walked him through the prayer that we say in our hearts before we say it with our lips, as millions have done before us. He gave me a hug, and left without a word.

When Mae showed up to relieve me a little before 8:00 I had two full bone-in hams in the oven and 10 dozen ears of fresh corn husked and ready to go in boiling water. I showed her the potato salad and the remaining several gallons of stew. Before her crew showed up we shared a quiet moment together at the counter, recounting the events of the day. As we spoke about the service, the rain, the change of wind direction, I finally gave her the news of Trent's conversion. Her eyes filled with tears, "Jib's up there dancing up a storm sharing the glory of God and celebrating another lost sheep come to the fold."

It took them ten days to mop up and declare the fire contained. Each day the presence of the fire crew diminished as they left for other fires in other forests and states. Glen and his friends returned with the wheel line to their own homes, Buck returned his herd to their regular pasture. Our new friends, with their shovels and parachutes, told us goodbye and left seeking new danger. Trent, among the last to go, made sure all the gear was packed, all the bills were paid, and his new family thanked before he pulled the plug. He promised to stay in touch.

What had been a curse, God had turned into a blessing. Where there had been fear, there was hope. Longtime friends were reunited having faced the fire together and with God's help, had overcome it.

Love grew from adversity, bringing Faith and Buford back together after years apart. They married the following spring. Not a life was lost, not a home was burned, the economy of the Widespot and indeed the entire valley flourished, and one man found salvation in Jesus. We hired a full time dishwasher, Buff became a full time cook, Faith helped Mae serve while the girls were in school, and I remain here welcoming such as you as you pass by.

PART FOUR

"Hello, I'm John Roberts, most folks call me Bum, can I get you something to eat? Biscuits and gravy, sure full or half? We make our own baking powder biscuits and I have fresh sausage gravy from this morning. Like eggs with it? Let me get back to where I can get to work," I said as I returned to the kitchen area after greeting a new guest. He looked to be in his late fifties or early sixties, clean and well groomed but poorly dressed. I could see a ten-year-old chevy pickup parked out front with an out-of-state license on it.

I continued to talk while he sipped his coffee, no other guests in the dining area. "Where you headed?" I asked.

"South, I guess," he replied. Well, us being just a short hop from the Canadian border, south gave him a lot of room to roam.

I let it go for a few minutes until he continued, "looking for work and a place to hang my hat."

"Oh, what do you do?" I asked, interested in his pedigree.

"Pretty much anything," he said, "I don't need much, something to fill the days and a little left over to live on."

"Over easy on the eggs?" I asked as they were ready to turn.

"Medium would be fine" he said. "Have you got a couple of links to go on the side? My wife always did up a couple of links for me."

"Sure 'nuff," I answered, "already have them on the plate." I turned the corner from the kitchen with a platter filled with biscuits and gravy, sausage, and two over medium. I set it in front of him, poured a refill, and asked about hot sauce or ketchup.

"No thanks," he said, "I have a bad stomach, can't eat the good stuff since they took my gall bladder." I noticed that black pepper wasn't among the things he'd been forced to give up.

"The locals have pretty much come and gone for the morning, we get a new crop around 11:00 and more in the evening," I said answering his unasked question. I had seen him look around the empty room.

"Mae, she's the owner, is usually here with me, but she's under the weather now, so I run it until the girl comes in to help at lunch time."

He nodded, head down, eating quietly.

"Might be some jobs at the mill in Sandpoint," I offered, "we hear the new owners have upgraded the equipment and are buying all the logs they can get."

"I taught at the university," he said quietly, "until my wife died. I couldn't stand to stay put with all the memories around me. Everywhere I went, we had gone together before. Everyone I met had that look of sympathy in their eyes. I couldn't have a conversation without them bringing up how sorry they were. I know they all meant well but it hurt just the same."

He continued, "I guess I want a clean slate, to make new memories and not have to share the old ones with anyone else." I nodded, not knowing what to add.

"Family?" I asked.

"Not really, a son on the east coast and a sister somewhere down south. I haven't seen her in years and he's too tied up in himself to care about me, he didn't even make his mother's funeral," he confided.

"Where ya stayin' tonight?" I asked, knowing that most of the cabins out back were vacant.

He stopped eating for a moment, "I hadn't really considered that. Probably in my truck, why do you ask?"

"We have a few cabins out back, don't rent them out regular, but they come in handy once in a while."

It looked at first like he might take offense, "I pay my own way, I don't need a hand out," he answered.

"Never figured any different," I replied quietly, "just an offer from a friend. A friend once did the same for me when I was passing through, goin' on six years now. It changed my life."

His look softened.

"More coffee?"

"Nope, thanks, two's my limit, enlarged prostate and all." I nodded, aware of the common condition among older men.

"What'd you teach?" I asked in an attempt to draw him into conversation.

I have a Doctor of Divinity, taught theology at a Bible College in Montana for twenty-eight years.

"Have you ever lead your own church?" I asked.

"No, unfortunately. I spent my life teaching others how it was done but never had the opportunity myself."

It occurred to me he hadn't volunteered his name so I stuck out my hand to him, "Bum, Bum Roberts."

He returned the greeting with, "Nate Walker, nice to meet you."

I returned to the kitchen area, getting things prepped for the lunch hour which was quickly approaching. Buffy, our other cook, would be joining me today since Mae was out, and his new wife Faith also, to wait the tables.

Mae had, three months before, tried to get out of bed one morning and found she'd had a stroke during the night. Although we had gotten her to the hospital right away, she still had weakness and lack of control on her left side. Since then she had come home and was making good progress, but still needed a walker or cane and tired quickly.

The janitor at the grade school and his wife Pam and their two had just come in and seated themselves.

"Too late for breakfast?" he asked.

"Never, Tom," I said with feeling, "meet my new friend Nate Walker."

Nate, this is Tom and Pam Green and their twin girls, Melissa and Melinda. Don't ask me which is which."

Nate got up and walked over, taking their hands and repeating his name again. They asked him to join them unless he was in a hurry, and to my surprise he did. He picked up his cup and plate and sat right down beside one of the twins, who eyed him suspiciously.

Tom ordered ham 'n' eggs, Pam and the girls burgers and fries.

"Enjoying the summer Tom?" I asked, knowing that school started again in less than a week.

"Yeah, it went by too fast, now I gotta go back to work."

One of the twins reached up and touched Nate's cheek carefully, having noticed the silver stubble on it.

"You a grandpa?" she asked bluntly.

Both Tom and Pam were embarrassed and tried quickly to make unnecessary amends, but Nate had already broken out in a grin.

"Sure am," he said, "but I have never seen my grandchildren, they live far away."

"Our grandpa is in Heaven," she offered solemnly, "we never see him either."

I delivered the food, brought drinks, and was returning to the kitchen when the newly weds came in the rear door.

Let me quickly bring you up to speed on them. Bufford, we call him Buffy, went to school with Faith. While still in grade school he had serious injuries from a bicycle accident that impaired his thought processes and held him back a grade or two in school. Meanwhile, Faith met and married a local, who was later killed in an accident, leaving her alone with three small girls.

By God's provision, I am certain, they were reintroduced last year during a big fire and subsequently married. I quickly introduced them to Nate before they went separate ways to make ready for the lunch hour. Mae joined us, leaning on a cane, looking slightly drawn but committed to sharing the load with us.

We had all attempted to dissuade her to no avail and had stopped, allowing her to do as she was able... mostly to run the register and hand orders to those at the counter. Nate looked up as she entered, catching her eye, then came over and introduced himself, "Nate Walker," he said with a smile, "a friend of Bum's. And you must be Mae."

Divine. I reminded myself to look up the definition sometime.

'Divine appointment' was what Pastor Jamison from Priest Lake called God's planned meetings. He was able to come up to our little country church every once in a while without feeling like he was abandoning his flock. Most of the time we met right here at the Widespot and did the best we could to honor God.

Mae gave me a look, indiscernible to me, but full of meaning none the less. I had no idea what she was thinking at that moment and had no time to ask as the crowd poured in, filling the tables.

"How's it going?" I asked Buff, who was topping burger buns with sauce and condiments while I turned the burgers and dropped fries into the oil.

"Good," he said, "we're just starting to feel like a family, it took a while for the girls not to see me as a replacement for their father. They acted terrible when we were first married, thinking that somehow I was the reason why their daddy wasn't coming home."

I nodded, understanding as an outsider the theory of the thing but not really relating to the emotion of it. "Glad to hear that you are all working it out," I said. "Ain't no easy thing replacing someone we love."

Bill Martin, our new County Sheriff, assumed his usual seat at the counter and accepted a menu from Mae, who gave me the usual smile. I threw on a corned beef on rye and dropped rings into the basket. Buffy had already filled a condiment cup with ranch dressing for him.

Bill was a deputy for several years before I came to the Widespot, ran for Sheriff last year when our Sheriff had retired and won by a landslide. More politics, more paperwork, more hours, and less police work he had complained when I had asked.

"Guess I'll try the corned beef on rye," he told Mae, "and rings rather than the fries, with a side of ranch." Mae handed me the order as I handed her the plate with a grin.

The new dishwasher joined us at about a quarter after one, as he did every day since Buff had been promoted to cook. He was a college kid trying to make a few bucks before going back to school in Moscow.

As the pace slowed, I asked Buff to hold down the fort before excusing myself to join Tom, Pam, Nate and the girls at their table.

"Nate," I said looking him square in the eye, "if you are not in a hurry, I'd like to show you something after things settle down in the kitchen that might interest you."

He nodded, "I have nothing but time," he said, "let me know when you are ready."

We traveled in his Silverado for several miles without speaking before he said, "where are we going?"

"We're here," I said, pointing across a field on the right. A short distance away was the country church building sitting off by itself. He seemed to consider what he was hearing as we pulled into the vacant lot in front of the church.

"Nice," he said appraisingly, "who keeps it up? It looks well kept."

"Several of the retired guys I think, guys who used to be deacons or elders or such."

"Looks like it has a full basement," he added.

"Yeah, it does, they held Sunday school for the kids there and Bible studies I am told.

"And," he said with a half smile... "why are you showing me this?"

I smiled back, "just wanted you to know that we are a God-loving, close knit family here that lacks a shepherd."

We drove back to the café, which looked nearly deserted now, most of our patrons having already gone.

"How long have you been a Christian?" he asked point blank.

"Nearly six years," I answered. "The second week I was here Jib, he was Mae's husband, helped me find Jesus.

"What denomination are you?" he asked, while watching for my reaction.

I knew what he meant, but played dumb. "Christian," I said with feeling.

"So you folks here have no church affiliation?" he asked again.

"Guess not, if you mean a name like Methodist, or Baptist or something... never thought it was necessary. Other folks must see it the same way, the name on the church is 'Country Church'.

"Is that offer still open for a cabin tonight?" he asked as we pulled into the parking lot.

"You can have Buffy's cabin," I said. "It's been vacant since he got married, it's right here next to mine." I took the key from under the mat and opened the door, hoping that Buff had left it in good order.

Inside it was neat as a pin, I should have known. Buffy was meticulous in his attention to detail when cleaning.

"What do you charge?" Nate asked.

"Mae don't usually charge folks," I said, "those who want to leave something put it in the fish bowl by the register inside, goes to helping those in need."

"I'll say tonight," he said matter-of-factly, getting his suitcase from his truck.

I was disappointed and maybe a little upset when I left my cabin and found that Nate's truck was gone. He had left early, before we were open, without opportunity to say goodbye. I had expected that I'd at least have opportunity to cook him breakfast before he headed 'south'.

I was still wrestling with my resentment when Mae joined me with a smile on her face and cane in her hand. I had already sliced the bone-in, and was running the boiled potatoes through the grater when she sat down at the counter with her morning cup.

"How's it goin' Bum?" she asked as she opened the morning paper.

"Okay, I guess," I answered, still feeling a heaviness in my spirit,

"Nate already left, didn't say a word." I guess I supposed getting it off my chest would relieve me of the burden I felt.

"I see that," she agreed, "he must be an early riser like Jib was.

Her appraisal of the man didn't help my attitude a bit. I let the subject drop and continued to ready the food for our morning guests while unlocking the doors and turning the Open sign. Do you ever wake up grumpy, not knowing why, with everything seeming to compound it as your day proceeds, until even good news lacks its luster? So began my day.

I've heard of this condition being described as a 'blue funk'. This senseless feeling of depression or despair. I've known those who live in it perpetually, lacking the ability to rise above it, that being termed as 'clinically depressed'. I am not such a case. I live daily with a sense of joy, an abounding faith in the future which God has chosen for me, and of the truth in His promises. What I'm saying here is that today was the exception. Upon reflection, perhaps a spiritual attack, the likes of which I seldom encounter.

As with many things, the 'mood magnifies reality', making every defeat greater and diminishing the joy of the victories. So the morning was a combination of frustrations, of mistakes, errors, and ungrateful and impatient guests, most of whom I saw daily and greatly loved.

My mood seemed contagious; Buffy hardly spoke, doing his job efficiently but without emotion. Faith joined Mae as they robotically did their jobs without their usual light-spirited conversation, serving and bussing tables. Resentment and irritation began to dominate my thoughts, extending finally to my co-workers in unreasonable ways.

Finally, Mae asked Faith and Buff to take a walk, giving us some time alone together.

"Bum Roberts," she began, not attempting to disguise her feelings.

"If Jib were here, he'd hit you along side the head, then he'd pray for you."

Then she stopped, looked me in the eye, and took me in her arms like a mother would have.

"Over five years now and I never saw you mean, what's goin' on in yer head?"

Had she not been holding me in her arms, I would have probably held on to my resentment and tried to make excuse, blaming others. As it was, I just dropped my shoulders, shook my head, and leveled with her. Then we prayed together and a great weight was lifted off me.

She laughed, "Then, you should have asked me, I coulda told ya. We visited last night for a long while. Nate's goin' down to Priest Lake to visit with Pastor Jamison, should be back tonight or tomorrow, he thinks God may be calling him to service."

Another lesson to file with many others about the workings of God and things in the spiritual realm. Satan, having no power over God and His plans, chose me instead, took me out of the equation, diminished my service. Had it not been for Mae, who knows what might have happened? I actually had fleeting thoughts of picking up my things and going on down the road. How foolish those thoughts seemed now.

Buff and Faith returned and I apologized to both, without going into detail, for my poor manners and bad mood. Both smiled the apology away with Buff giving me a hug.

PART FIVE

Lunch went well, the regulars joined us, bringing with them their stories of the day, and a few strangers like yourself remaining to get acquainted. "Where are you headin'? I'm John Roberts, everyone calls me Bum... what can I get you?"

Some folks think they can commune with God solely outside the presence of others. I'm here to tell you that both God's Word, and Bum Roberts, says that is wrong. We need each other, we need the wisdom and strength that God provides to us through our relationships with each other. We learn from and teach one another constantly the valuable lessons needed to stay strong in the faith.

A man might feel closer to God sitting on a rock in the wilderness, viewing His great creation, but in reality He is with us all the time, in every moment, sharing our joys and sorrows with us. My many friends are my greatest blessings, without whom my life would be less valuable.

"Single or double, fries or onion rings? Yeah, we cut our own, homemade. Let me get them on and I'll bring you something to drink, I see Mae's got her hands full over there."

I put on a double, grilled a couple slices of yellow onion, and topped a sesame bun while the fries cooked. Big fella, not only tall but wide. Almost Buck's size only heavier around the middle. Said he's going to Lewiston for a job at the mill. I've heard the folks down there joke that the putrid smell caused by the paper pulp is the smell of money. It comes from the mill. They process logs and lumber, sending them down the Columbia through the locks plumb to the ocean, grain from the high plains above Lewiston too.

"Here you are Bob, chocolate shake?"

"Sure," he said as I turned toward the ice-cream freezer with a big stainless steel mixing cup in my hand. It was after two o'clock when Faith hugged Buff and headed home to meet the girls. School is back in for the fall and they get off the bus at about three. We have not been back on a regular routine for some time now, first the big fire, then the thing with Mae's stroke. It's not clear yet how God has things planned out, so we try and stay flexible.

Our business had doubled since last year this time, thank you Lord, making it necessary to give Buff full time and a couple of raises. The folks around here love him and are so happy for Faith and the girls that God provided for them.

I've had a brisket soaking in pickling spices for a couple of days now. I plan to bake it slow, making it 'fall apart' tender, then serve it with cabbage and potatoes as corned beef and cabbage for our evening meal. When it gets a little cooler I may do the same, then boil it all together as a soup rather than slicing it.

"Good luck with the job, Bob... thanks for stopping by. Drive safely now," I said as my new friend left for his car.

Have you ever noticed that when you first meet someone, how they look seems really important? Later on, if you get to know them, you hardly notice that part at all. Did I tell you that Mae's husband Jib was a black man? Well, he was, and a big man too. First thing I noticed though, was his eyes, he had kind eyes. Wouldn't surprise me if that's what first got Mae's attention too. Too bad, I think, that we don't meet folks first time in the dark and get to know them before we see them and start to judge them by their looks.

'Bum-wisdom', that's what Mae calls the kind of stuff I just told you. I'm not sure whether it is a compliment or a joke, maybe both.

I went into the back and found that Buff was scolding our new dishwasher a bit for not taking more time to make sure it was done right. He never gets angry or mean, but sometimes explains a thing to death, making sure he's understood. He gave me a smile and a wink, then proceeded to bring me up to speed on where we stood with dinner.

Today was his short day, working through lunch and leaving before dinner, unless we have something special going on. He likes to spend evenings with his new family and we are happy to accommodate him as we can.

Parker house rolls, that's what my mom's generation called them. I suppose you could 'google' them and find out the history if you choose. When Mae is up to it, she does the baking, often sour dough, but once in a while these as well. I've got two full sheets of them rising, nearly ready to put into the ovens to serve with supper.

'Supper', there's another word that fits with the Parker house roll thing, something left over from past generations. Somehow it seems a little more personal to me than 'dinner', kind of like a house and a home. One's a little more comfortable feeling than the other, like shoes and slippers, I expect.

"Thanks," I said, sitting down with an iced tea beside Mae at the counter. She played dumb, but knew just what I meant. I could tell by the twinkle in those old eyes.

"For being my friend and loving me, for getting my head back on straight, for praying away my 'blue funk.'"

At that she laughed and said, "I haven't heard that in a while."

At a quarter till four the front door opened and disgorged the rotund body of Pastor Jamison into the room, followed by his wife, and Nate Williams.

I'm not sure I ever heard his first name. No one called him anything but pastor or Pastor Jamison in the time I had known him. He was nearly round, to the point one might wonder if he could fall down at all. Short stubby arms and legs seemed to indicate just where his shoulders and hips were.

He was well under six feet and possibly three hundred or so pounds with deep set twinkling blue eyes, round cheeks with huge dimples, and a jack-o-lantern smile that lit up the room. His counterpart was a slight built woman, with reddish hair, and a diminutive look about her. Almost as if he filled up the room leaving little space for her to exist. All were smiling as they entered and sat, first trying a booth, then a table, when Jamison wouldn't fit. He thought it was hilarious, and accused us of moving them closer together since he had been here a month ago.

Mae took them water and they asked us both to join them if we had time. I forgot to tell you, Pastor Jamison is a Southern Baptist by affiliation but probably too much of a renegade to fit their definition, any more than he could in one of our booths. He preaches straight Bible, nothing else, and a little on the critical side of many of the new Bible versions seeming to come out daily. I settled back, feeling slightly amused, content to let them bring the conversation to us.

Jamison began, turning his round head in my direction, "Nathan here tells me you are bent on replacing me," he said accusingly, before breaking out into a grin.

He continued, looking serious, "I worried when Jib passed and you picked up the brick that you might start bad mouthing me."

I struggled to remain silent as he continued to enjoy his humorous tirade. "Well," he said, "you have gotten your way. You and this Nate character can run it your way, I quit."

I paused for effect, then answered him, "it's about time, by the way, why are you telling me? I'm not in leadership of the church. As a matter of fact, I wonder who is?"

After the banter stopped, Jamison provided names and numbers for the group that held responsibility for upkeep and maintenance on the building to Nate. It appeared that they intended to try and meet with them yet today to pass the baton.

It was nearing 4:00 when I returned to the kitchen, still shaking my head mentally at the workings of the Lord. Thirty-six hours ago I had never met Nate, 24 hours ago he was searching for something to fill the loneliness in his heart, 12 hours ago he had never met Jamison. And now, it seemed he might be the Lord's answer to many prayers and we the answer to his.

They left, saying that they'd be back for dinner after meeting with the Board, just as the first of the crowd seated themselves. We plated about 35 meals of corned beef and cabbage and another dozen or so off the menu by the time God's servants returned about 6:00, all smiles.

They took a table and ordered four specials, Mae served them water and drinks, while I plated the meals and set out a platter of her rolls and butter for the table. Only two other tables of the dinner crowd remained, I gave them refills and offered them our dessert choices. Tom and Pam and their twin daughters ordered sundaes; two strawberry and two chocolate. The other table deferred, claiming no room for more.

Our young dishwasher bussed the remaining dishes and loaded them in the machine while I fried a double burger and fries with a chocolate shake for him to take with him. He had classes three days a week in Coeur d'Alene but spent the rest of the week here with his family and working with us.

I noticed that Mae had joined the table after delivering their meals, her left leg bothering her no doubt. I turned the Open sign at 6:30 and shut down the grill after bricking it clean.

"Join us!" came the call from the floor, Jamison not shy to use his baritone voice. I did, grateful to be off my feet, sipping a cold iced tea and nibbling on fries after I had pulled up another chair.

"The Board liked the idea of hiring Nate," Jamison bragged. "They are paying him the same as they have you and I.

"But," I complained, "we are seasoned vets, this is his first church, hardly seems fair to me."

"He's on probation," Jamison said, "they'll likely cut his pay once they've heard him preach."

Nate was taking it all good naturedly, eating and smiling.

He finally spoke, "they may be paying me what I'm worth," he ventured humbly. "It's anyone's guess how God may use me from the pulpit."

I had to take one more poke at my new friend. "Don't worry, God is long suffering," I said, "He's put up with me the best part of five years now."

I felt Mae wince when she thought back to when Jib had held service, had it really been that long ago? Had she really been alone that long?

Nate spoke again. "I have a fifth-wheel still in Montana. Can you put me up in the cabin until after Sunday service? If so, I'll have a week to go get it and return before the next service. I'm thinking I can live in it at the church until I get my feet on the ground and see if you folks want to keep me."

Mae smiled, "that would be our great pleasure," she said a little too sincerely.

I mentioned when I first spoke to you folks that God gave me certain insight. It was telling me now, as it had during the fire with Buff and Faith, that a spark had been lit.

A day that had for me started on a low note, was closing on a high, praise God, I thought. It was a Wednesday night, middle of the week, halfway day for those who had weekends off.

The Jamison's, who had a long drive home, finished eating and said their goodbyes, promising to try and make it back for a Sunday service now and then. We stayed on for a few minutes at the table, finally Mae spoke.

"Whatcha think, Bum, maybe the fish bowl could finance a little reception for our new pastor, it'd give folks a chance to meet him and get the word out for Sunday?"

"You're the boss Mae," I said. "You work out the wrinkles and make some calls and I'll order and cook the food."

Nate started to object, but his efforts were in vain, it was a done deal. The three of us sat there alone for a few more minutes, then I began to feel uncomfortable for some reason.

I broke the ice, "so Nate, now that you are officially our new shepherd, what would you prefer that we call you?" I assumed that it was his change of station that had put us ill at ease. He seemed surprised by the question and had no ready answer.

Finally he spoke, "well, I have never considered it. You called Jamison 'Pastor Jamison' and while that does show respect for his position, it seems a little stuffy to me. I am not crazy about my full name Nathan, never have been, but my mother chose it because he was a prophet who was faithful to God and feared no man. Does 'Pastor Nate' seem too informal to you?"

"I'm comfortable with it," I said, "but I might slip and just call you Nate if we're fishing. How about you, Mae?"

"I like Nate, I mean, Pastor Nate," she said reddening noticeably.

I was chuckling right along with my old friend Jib. I know you do, I thought. If Nate caught the slip he didn't indicate it.

"Okay then, we'll go with 'Pastor Nate' and let folks call me whatever is comfortable for them."

"What is your favorite meal, Pastor Nate?" I asked him with emphasis on the name. He did not hesitate a beat.

"Barbecue, any kind of barbecue," he answered.

"Done!" I said, turning toward Mae. "How about both chicken and ribs?"

"Were you thinking Friday night or Saturday?" I continued.

"I think Saturday at the church, we can use the basement or outside in the parking lot depending on the turnout and the weather," she replied.

I could see she had already given it some thought. I nodded. "I'll call Al in the morning and see what he has on hand in the way of meat. Were you figuring to make it a potluck with us doing just the meat and have folks bring something, or do the whole thing?"

"Let's do it all this time," she answered, "just like we did during the fire. After Nate, Pastor Nate, gets his feet on the ground he will have plenty of time to arrange church activities for himself."

Nate was looking at her as if seeing her for the first time. "Thank you," he said, "you are very thoughtful and gracious."

As the moment passed, I got up and retrieved a pad of paper from the office and began to write a menu and shopping list. I knew we had over two hundred paper plates in storage left over from the fire, likewise plastic ware and napkins. Thank you God and Trent I said mentally. The church had plenty of folding chairs and tables. I began the list... ribs, chicken, potato salad, macaroni salad, coleslaw, rolls, butter, punch, lemonade, coffee, paper cups and ice. I slid the list over to the other two, "see anything I missed?"

They looked it over, and then Mae said, "how about dessert?"

"Yeah, I forgot that. What do you think, maybe cobbler, apple, berry, or cherry?"

"Probably all three," Mae answered. "Remember, we have to use pans that will fit in the church ovens to stay hot, and I'll make sure the church freezer has room for ice cream as well.

Nate was quiet as he continued to listen to us devising our battle strategy. "Strawberry rhubarb," he said softly to himself, "she always made strawberry rhubarb." He had a faraway look in his eyes, reliving a happier time, the 'she' no doubt referred to his late wife.

When he returned to us, he had tears in his eyes. He simply said, "I'm sorry, I was just remembering the last time I was at a church gathering." Mae covered his hand with hers, but said nothing.

Thursday morning arrived like any other, with the sun peeking over the mountains, high white sirius clouds gracing the clear blue morning sky, with just a hint of the coming fall in the air. We had not had our first frost yet; consequently the leaves remained green, awaiting God's signal to blossom into shades of red, yellow, and orange. But the hint was there to those who had counted years by the changing seasons, unmistakable and irresistible. Mae and I visited over coffee while I prepared for the breakfast meal as usual. "How many," I asked, "how many do you expect will come?"

"A free meal and a chance to lay eyes on the new preacher," she answered as if it was self-evident, "I'll bet no less than 150."

"Can we handle that," I asked?

"Nope, we can't, not with our crew," she said, "but God can and I'm hopin' He'll give us a hand."

She continued, "I'm going to call some of the ones who helped us during the fire and ask them to help out.

I nodded. "One hundred-fifty it is, done deal."

I called Al, ordered 75 lbs of cut up chicken, and 100 lbs of ribs, half pork, and half beef, fifty lbs of red potatoes, six heads of green and one purple cabbage, an extra gallon of Hellman's, and a flat of lemons. The commissary filled in the blank slots for me rounding out our deficiencies in the menu, including makings for the barbecue sauce and desserts.

Tom, our ISP friend, joined us for breakfast remarking that he had already heard news of the reception from several. Buffy, Faith, and our dishwasher helped make the morning flow smoothly.

One after another, the locals came and went, most repeating the same message, all committed to attending. By the time we were bussing the last of the tables my unofficial count was fifty, including those who had eaten but not their families at home. The commissary made their delivery right after lunch.

During the slack between meals, I usually prepped for the next meal. Today, I let Buff take the lead while I began to make the barbecue sauce, coleslaw dressing, and organize for Al's delivery which arrived a little after 2:00.

I have no idea how real chefs are taught to do barbeque, my guess is that there are as many ways as you have cooks, with each standing firmly by their personal choice.

I chose to boil all of the meat, separately of course, saving the valuable broth for use later. About 45 minutes at a rapid boil gave me a guarantee that it was fully cooked. Each was then drained and heavily seasoned as it cooled and continued to drain, then submerged in a barbecue sauce of my own making, to rest overnight in the cooler before being charcoal barbequed Saturday morning.

The meat done, I took a break while listening to Mae talking on the phone, spreading the word and recruiting volunteers. The women of the church still had the remnants of a sewing circle and were willing to help with the table dressing after the men had set them up.

Mae put down the phone long enough to smile and say that we could count on 20 volunteers to help. I boiled and drained the macaroni before assembling it into a salad which was stored in the cooler beside the coleslaw. I had held off on the potato salad, preferring to do it Friday to keep it from drying out as it soaked up the mayonnaise.

Buffy had baked a whole ham, planning on serving it as a special for our dinner meal with anything left over to go into au gratin potatoes on Friday. He had made it easy for me to prepare for Saturday while covering the bases today and tomorrow. I thanked and complimented him before he and Faith left for home.

It was not until just now that I noticed I had not seen Nate all day. He had not been in at breakfast or lunch. I mentioned it to Mae who acquired a puzzled look before promising to check on him. It was after 3:00 when she advised me that his pickup was gone but his personal things were still in the cabin.

Once again, I felt the old Enemy trying to make Nate's absence personal, causing me to be resentful. This time I prayed and shed my animosity like a worthless coat. About 4:00 Pastor Nate came in the front door all smiles, full of life and enthusiasm. He sat at the counter beside Mae who was rolling napkins and began telling us of his day.

He had been at the church, praying, surveying, writing his sermon, walking the grounds asking for God's blessings over every square foot. He'd risen before daylight and spoke of a 'glorious communion' with the Lord over that entire time. I felt ashamed to the point of nearly apologizing to him, but thought better of it. Instead I asked the Lord for forgiveness.

Our dinner hour lasted two, with many whom we had not seen recently coming to discuss and get more details about our new pastor. He was on hand to meet and greet many personally. My feeling was one of a thirsty community long deprived of a spiritual leader finally finding water gushing from a rock in the form of Pastor Nate.

Our very unofficial count was well over a hundred now with still two days to go. I was beginning to worry. I used commercial 5:1 syrup to make both the lemonade, adding a half dozen juiced lemons and their rinds and a quart of pineapple juice; and the punch, five gallons of each. My focus was on the Saturday meal, luckily Buffy had made my job easier by his efficient use of the ham Thursday.

Mae began the assault Friday morning before I came in, having two sheet pans of rolls in the oven when I arrived. You could have gained several pounds just from breathing the air. Sheriff Bill joined us, forgoing his usual, choosing instead to try biscuits and gravy on his way to his office. He confirmed that he and his family were planning to attend both Saturday's food fest and worship on Sunday.

I learned that Bill was an elder, one of those who had kept the building in good repair for the last several years. It was ditto, a few minutes after Bill left when Buck and Thomas, his eldest, stopped by for breakfast. And so it went through the morning and into the lunch hour.

I called Al after lunch had died down and ordered a 15 lb pork butt which he promised to deliver right away. I had given up trying to keep count when Mae took her break and asked how we were doing.

I answered, "I gave up at 150 and ordered more meat. We now are also serving pulled pork sandwiches."

She laughed, "oh ye of little faith," then continued to brush the top of her rolls with melted butter. Our dinner hour was light, thank you Lord, giving us a chance to clean up early in preparation for a big day Saturday. At 7:00, closed and tired, I put the heavily seasoned butt into the oven at 225º, expecting to cook it all night, covered with foil but only minimal water.

The Widespot owns a half dozen electric roasting pans, each having a capacity of about four and a half gallons. It was our plan to utilize them to keep the barbecued meats hot in them, use them for transport, and then serve from them once at the church.

About 7:00 a.m. I took the butt from the oven, very pleased with the look of it. After allowing it to cool for an hour I began the process of "pulling" it, or breaking it down to serve. It made a mountain of stringy, moist and delicious meat that was immediately bathed in barbecue sauce, before resting in a warm roaster.

Mae had planned the dinner hour from 4:00 to 6:00, meaning that we should be there and ready to go by 3:00. Buffy joined me, and filled and then lit the big barbecue outside. While we waited for it to burn down, we checked one item after another off our list, mentally setting the tables, setting up the food line, running extension cords for the roasters, icing the salads, sitting up the drinks, right down to dipping the ice cream for the dessert. Every item had to be taken with us since the church kitchen had not been inventoried in years and could not be depended on. Every cup, ladle, spoon, knife, cutting board, apron, ice chest, or paper cup must be loaded and delivered along with the food.

By the time the charcoal was ready for the meat, Buffy had Jib's old pickup piled high with non-food items. As we checked things off the list, new ones were added. When he left with the first load, I began to put the ribs over the fire to reheat and get the "burn" on them that people enjoyed.

As the sugar caramelized and turned color they were turned once before going to the cutting board where I broke them down with a butcher's knife into individual ribs, then placed them in a warm roaster.

I repeated this process over and over until we had three full roasting pans full of ribs ready to serve.

Two of Mae's male volunteers returned with Buff in the old truck for a second load while I cleaned the grill before adding more charcoal to the fire. I duplicated my earlier efforts, this time with the chicken which was moister and thicker, which took a little longer to cook. Praise God, things went more quickly than anticipated. By 2:00 we had nearly everything either already delivered or in the truck ready to deliver. Mae called repeatedly reminding us to bring X, Y, and Z when we came while filling us in on their progress.

When we arrived with the final load I could see nothing but a well-planned and well organized mass of tables and people waiting for guests. Nate and Mae were working side by side laughing, talking, and situating tables in the work areas. At 3:00 we actually began setting out the food, drinks, and consumables except those being kept on ice. We had, of course, forgotten several items including the cobblers, the ice cream, plastic spoons, and paper bowls to serve it in. The easy-ups from our parking lot vendors had been relocated, providing shade for the serving area.

Pastor Nate thanked everyone present, then asked the volunteers to join him in prayer for God's blessing upon the day, the event, and the new chapter beginning today in his life. He was still wearing his apron as he began meeting and greeting our guests about 4:00, some new to the church, other past members and committed patrons. Like the Widespot, the church had many stories to tell if one had the time and interest to hear them. Our first guests through the line were of course, starving teenagers who arrived in groups, both with and without parents. We knew many of them from the restaurant.

Enterprising Mae found a legal pad and pen which she insisted everyone use to register as guests with a column for phone numbers. Many of us could see through her attempt to have a way to re-contact the guests and invite them to church service. As more and more arrived and the food line formed, even a couple of passing motorists were waved in by the crowd and joined in. As the dining tables filled, the volunteer servers took time to ask a blessing for each table.

With tables both inside and out, our guests could either enjoy or avoid the warm fall afternoon as they choose. I encouraged Buffy to join his little family at a table before returning to help me dish barbeque as the number of guests increased dramatically about 5:00. Mae I noticed, had discarded her cane and was not noticeably even limping until late in the evening. Al, Mary, and Blake, Buck, Meg, and the boys, Tom and Hazel, Bill and Sally, Jim the grocer and his family, our postman, Don and wife, and even old Sadie Hawkins were among the many regulars from the Widespot who joined us.

In addition, Glen Gardner and several of his farmer friends with their families came to visit and eat. Tom, Pam and the twins were among the first to come and last to leave, seeming to enjoy the fellowship as much as the food. Just as it seemed that the stream of guests had stopped, Pastor Jamison and his family made their entrance, giving a short speech reminiscent of Moses turning over the leadership to Joshua.

I whispered to Buff as they took their seats at a table with plates laden, that I'd like to see an 'eat off' between the Spellmans and the Jamisons. He could hardly stop laughing having just watched each take two plates, one for meat, the other for salads. Mae continued to man the guest register and refused several offers to contribute for the meal, saying "save it for tomorrow's worship service."

We began to cover and pull the dinner items from the tables, replacing them with the dessert at about 5:30, but left them accessible for late comers, serving staff, and for those who wanted to take some home. By now Pastor Nate had made the rounds of the tables and was offering seconds or desserts to the timid, scoring points for his friendly servants' attitude. Most were still seated as the sun dropped behind the mountain tops and the long twilight of the autumn evening began.

Sunday morning seemed to come early. Even without the need to open the Widespot to customers, there was a church service to attend and plenty of cleanup left from the night before. Over coffee, Mae and I discussed the benefit of not needing to open the café any longer on Sundays to attract guests to church service. We both liked the idea of a day off each week to worship and relax.

In the past and according to the marquee out in front, the church service began at 11:00. Pastor Nate had seen no reason to change it and was waiting for us when we arrived at 10:30. He greeted us warmly, thanking us for the previous day's effort to introduce him to the community, as though it were he and not we who were being served. He took Mae aside and asked if she played piano, which she did not, but offered the names of a couple who did, Faith among them. I myself had only attended the church a few times when Pastor Jamison came and I was able to break free at the café.

I admired the craftsmanship that someone had built into the building; strong, stout, and durable rather than ornate and decorative. My guess, it was built by men with a sense of permanence and not design. It showed little of a woman's hand and nothing of an architect's imagination. It had withstood the ravages of time since the beginning of the 20th century, looking none the less for wear.

We had been seated only a few minutes when cars began to arrive and pour out God's people. Nate greeted every one personally, shaking hands and reliving meetings from the previous afternoon before allowing them to enter and be seated. He gave no appearance of feeling rushed, even as the guests began to back up outside and the clock moved toward the hour. At 11:10 he closed one of the double doors, leaving the other ajar, then walked forward up the center isle to the lectern on the raised dais at center stage.

"Good morning," he said with obvious sincerity in his voice, "it is so nice to see so many friends from yesterday afternoon once again." Amens echoed.

"My first order of business today is to praise the Lord God for this, my first opportunity to pastor a church." The crowd was attentive as he retold the same story as he had previously told me. His days teaching, his married life and the loss of his wife, and the answer to his prayers that God had provided in making this church available to fill the loneliness in his heart.

He shared with the congregation his plans to bring back his fifth wheel and live in it until he could find permanent quarters, that his door was always open, or would be when fully settled, and his desire to become a participating member of the community. He stopped and fielded questions from the floor for several minutes before asking one of his own.

"Do we have someone willing and able to play piano?" Two or three hands were raised, including Faith's.

"And... what are your thoughts about a standing worship group?"

Again, hands went up with ideas, but he continued... "too many times I have seen more emphasis put on the quality of worship music to the detriment of the purpose of it. I care not how well you sing as much as that your heart is in it." Heads nodded agreement.

"Our team is not here to entertain us but to make a joyful noise unto the Lord." Some laughed, several amen'd, while others just smiled.

"Those interested in music please come see me after service," he added.

He began his sermon by returning to speak of himself. "I'm a small town guy, just like most of you. I chose that way of life purposely, calling Montana rather than New York my home. While it is not always the case, small communities seem to have a less worldly value system than larger ones. Many times this only becomes apparent in times of adversity like the fire by which you were recently threatened. At all times we should turn to God for strength and support, but unfortunately we often look to ourselves first."

"I was privileged to hear of God's answer to your corporate prayer that was not by any means just good fortune as some might claim. We must learn to pray with faith and conviction and expect God to both hear and answer. We, however, cannot order it up like you can at the Widespot." That brought a laugh and some hoots. "God answers in His own way and in His own time."

As I looked around, the crowd was enwrapped in his words, attentive and eager to hear more.

He stopped speaking and led us in prayer before asking us to open up our Bibles. "Do you think it is coincidence that God begins the story of creation with 'in the beginning'?" he asked, before going on to clarify why he had asked.

"Think for a moment when your children were very young and you were telling them a bedtime story that always began with 'once upon a time'. Everything in creation, except God, has a beginning and an end. Our minds are programmed to be finite, we have no concept of infinite, God is attempting to enlarge our borders and give us a vision of the eternity of which we will someday be a part."

He continued to speak without a microphone, in a common sense tone of voice, for nearly an hour before he stopped. "Please forgive my message this morning," he said. "I feel as though I was poorly prepared. If you'll read the book of John for next week, with special emphasis on the first ten verses, we'll get to know God and each other better." He closed us in prayer after announcing that next week we would include worship in our service.

As we stood to leave, groups were clustered about smiling and talking. There was a clear feeling of goodwill in the air. Faith and two others had buttonholed Pastor Nate, apparently eager to be considered for the position of playing piano. I overheard Tom and Hazel invite Nate to join them for dinner during the coming week, but he expressed his regrets as he planned to leave tomorrow for Montana and would be traveling most of the week.

Family after family took their turn spending a few minutes with their new pastor before heading home. Finally, it was just the three of us left in the empty sanctuary, with me waiting on Mae to give her a lift home. Finally I got the hint, duh. I asked Pastor Nate, "would you mind giving Mae a lift back to the Widespot, I have some cleanup I need to get done before morning."

"Of course," he said pleasantly, "I'm headed that way myself as soon as I lock up." Mae was smiling as I left.

After I had changed my clothes, I found myself alone, with no plans at all for the day. Like a magnet, the café drew me back inside and before long I was busy cleaning up roasting pans and putting things away. We had plenty of leftovers from last night ready for tomorrow's lunch. I saw that as a blessing. An hour later the Silverado arrived with Nate and Mae aboard.

How far ahead do you think God plans? A week, a year, ten years, a life time? That was the thought on my mind, having considered what I heard Pastor Nate preach this morning. "In the beginning..."

When was the beginning for the story that was seeming to be playing itself out right before my eyes? When did God know that Jib would die leaving Mae alone or Nate's wife leaving him crushed and empty? How far ahead did He make the plan to fill the vacancy at our church? And... which things seeming so hopeless to us today will turn around and produce joy tomorrow?

PART SIX

The day dawned overcast, and such is the way in the mountains, the seasons ending and beginning like the edge of a sheer rock cliff. At six o'clock the grey sky held the promise of rain, one could almost taste it. There is something unique about the smell of pregnant clouds, like that of wet leather when held close to your nose, or like the decaying smell of wood you might find deep in old growth forests, not unpleasant at all, but unique in its strangeness.

Mamas and Papas... from the 60's, something comes to memory about 'Monday, Monday' I thought as I put on the coffee and fired up the flattop. I put a pot of water on to boil for the potatoes to become hash browns, and turned on the lights and vent fan. This Monday, who and what will it bring today? What story will I have to tell a stranger passing through? What material did God write a thousand years before I was born that I might share?

My mood was thoughtful. I was happy, content, feeling fulfilled and refreshed after a long day of labor on Saturday and one of rest on Sunday. Mae had not yet made her appearance, but I knew she would show up any time now with her newspaper. I turned the Open sign early, to surprise Tom mostly, not expecting travelers this early.

We were out of bone-in, so I sliced some nice 'water added' steaks for the breakfast crowd, feeling a little guilty as I did so. Pressed ham, no matter how good, never comes close to the real thing once grilled. I noted the need for several on my meat order.

The potatoes were boiled and softened so I ran cold water over them to cool and set them up. In a few minutes I would drain and run them through the grater for hash browns, lemon juice added to the water would keep them from turning brown. Mae breezed in, without her cane and without her morning paper, looking rested and happy. I poured us a cup and made a comment on how well the dinner went and the Sunday service also. She agreed, then sat beside me sipping the hot black liquid, before speaking.

"He's leaving today for Montana," she said, as though I hadn't already known. He, of course referred to Nate, although she hadn't said so. I nodded, remembering him saying so previously, then again during the service.

"He'll likely be gone a couple of days at least," she added. I nodded but said nothing. I could see that my silence was unsettling to her, so I made comment, "it's a long trip pulling a trailer."

You have to know I was having fun with all of this. She finally gave up and came right out with it.

"He asked if I'd like to ride along." I wasn't at all surprised, but feigned it. "Oh?"

"Well, what do you think? How would it look to folks? Do you think it's alright?" she said all at once, showing her frustration.

I hesitated, then smiled and said, "you are both adults, Christians, and the ride might be good for both of you. I wouldn't worry about reputations, no one needs to know and if they do, so what, you are who you are and folks love you for it. The heck with any others with wagging tongues."

"A single caution though, the folks there who knew he and his wife as a couple may not be as kind to either of you."

Mae seemed to understand when she replied, "you are right, never gave that much thought, maybe Nate and I need to discuss it."

"Well, my love," I said in all sincerity, "either way I approve and so would Jib." She gave me a hug and a million dollar smile, before literally skipping out.

I had fixed breakfast for Tom who was making the rounds with today's mail, and a couple on their way to Spokane sat together in the corner booth eating when Buffy and Faith came in the rear door. We shared "mornings" then went to work getting things ready for the 'thundering herd' that may or may not arrive hungry.

A few minutes later Nate and Mae entered together, she donning an apron and he taking a seat at the counter. I poured him a cup and handed him a menu, "a bite to eat before you leave?" I asked.

He smiled, "yeah, my regular." I had to laugh, he hadn't been in town a week and already he had "a regular." Biscuits and gravy with two little piggies and two eggs over medium had been his order in the few days we had known each other so I readied them and put them on a plate.

The Spokane folks left quickly after eating, going straight to their car and having missed a stop at the register. I saw Mae smile as she tucked their ticket away in her pocket and bussed the table. Good way to begin the day I thought, "paying it forward." That being one of my favorite movies, and one of the few I owned, I relived a few special moments from it from memory.

Nearly every one of the regulars was happy to see Nate and many made a point to come over and compliment him on his sermon.

As I refilled his coffee I said quietly, "wasn't so great... last time I preached God turned on the rain and changed the wind to put the fire out."

He laughed out loud and then answered, "you are a hard act to follow. I'll give next week's sermon more thought."

At 10:30 a stranger walked in joining Nate at the counter, sitting a couple of stools away. Let me share an observation I have made over the years. If you have twelve men and twelve chairs they will look for a place to sit besides the obvious one. Men, normal men, not homophobes, are reluctant to sit beside one another. What do you suppose that is about? Anyway, Mr. Stranger sitting two doors down apparently liked the look of Nate's meal and ordered the "same."

Mae delivered his breakfast, refilled his coffee and asked, "where you headed?" just as she had asked me years ago.

"I'm hitchin'" he said, "car gave out on the long grade out of Lewiston, overheated, then threw a rod." He continued, "I have folks in Bonners Ferry, if I can get there I have a place to stay until I can find work."

"What do you do?" she asked him.

"I was a millwright," he said, "but nearly everything is going automated now with computers and we are a dying breed."

"Enjoy your breakfast," she said refilling his coffee.

Then turning to Nate, speaking quietly, she asked, "how far out of your way is Bonners Ferry on your way to Montana?"

"Not much, I can take US Highway 2 across to Libby, then south, why?"

She sat down next to him, "I've been thinking about your offer to ride with you to bring back the trailer. I am tempted to go, to enjoy your company, to get away for a couple of days, and for us to get to know each other better. On the other hand, I am a little concerned at what your old friends and neighbors might think when we arrive together. I wonder if God has not provided this young man, needing a ride north, as His answer to your desire for a traveling companion."

He looked at first as though he was ready to do battle, to defend himself against any accusation or gossip or defend their honor against his friends. But then he seemed to pause and consider what she had just said.

"You know, people being what they are in our fallen world, you could be right. Our friends, meaning my wife's and mine, are still hurting from the loss too. They could easily say or do something hurtful without meaning to, I hadn't considered that."

Mae nodded, "hopefully we'll have lots of time to get to know each other," she said.

Mae introduced Nate to the young traveler, leaving them alone to visit, while she serviced the other tables. Nate and Tim Henson left heading north a little before 11:00, heading to Bonners Ferry.

As she delivered the first lunch order to the wheel, she gave me a melancholy smile and said, "beyond your years."

I puzzled at her meaning as I loaded a couple of plates with today's special, pulled pork and salad, also left over from the reception. Buff and I were cookin' both literally and figuratively, with nearly all the tables filled by noon. Both Mae and Faith were scampering just to keep up. Buck came in alone, for the first time in memory, and sat at the counter without his usual fanfare, causing me to ask, "you feelin' alright, Buck?"

"Yeah, fine," he answered, "just in a hurry! Got a cow down and need to see the vet. Have any of those ribs left from yesterday that you can bundle up to go?"

I had several cardboard chicken buckets on the back shelf left over from when we used to have a braiser. I hit the ribs a lick in the microwave to knock off the chill and filled the bucket to the top with what we had left, both beef and pork. I handed the bucket to him with a roll of paper towels before sending him on his way with a worried smile.

Nate and Tim visited as they traveled, Nate trying to get a feel for Tim's spiritual health, Tim glad to have a ride and companionship. Tim, now in his mid-thirties, had set chokers for the high line loggers, fallen trees for smaller outfits, driven trucks, and maintained equipment before going to the mill. He had never been married, had served three tours in Iraq, and believed in God but only knew Jesus Christ as a name poorly used in logging camps.

Since he seemed open and interested, Nate gave his own witness, explaining it as he went. By the time they hit the city limits of Bonners Ferry and encountered road construction, they had become friends.

When Nate offered to extend their road trip to include a little detour through Montana, Tim made a quick phone call to his mother to update her, then settled into the seat with apparent excitement.

Our evening meal rush was over and we were cleaning up when Buck stopped in on his way home.

"Staple", he declared, "vet said she'd picked up a staple in her feed. We'd have lost her had we waited longer. It was in her rumen with a bunch of other junk the magnet had picked up and was beginning to block the passage of food into her stomach."

For those of us who were not cowboys, he continued to explain how God had created cows with two stomachs and that the practice of having them swallow strong magnets to catch unwanted metal was normal.

"Thanks for the ribs, Bum," he said, "they really hit the spot."

"Yer welcome," I shouted after him as he left for home and dinner no doubt.

I had just finishing mopping the kitchen, bricked the grill and turned off the heat to the fryers when I saw Mae sit at the bar with her usual iced tea. I joined her, saying nothing at first, then asked what "beyond your years" was supposed to mean.

"Wise, silly," she answered, "wise beyond your years." It's an old saying when someone young gives sage advice beyond what one might expect of them. I took it as a compliment then.

"You do have the gift of insight don't you?" she said. I sipped my tea and answered her, "sometimes."

I thought back to last year when I had seen the spark lit between Buffy and Faith, I was seeing it again now between Nate and Mae.

Pastor Nate, I have to get used to addressing him properly, made it back to us safely on Saturday afternoon. He pulled into the Widespot about 2:00 to say hello, before continuing on to set up his new home behind the church building. Our lunch crowd gone, Mae finished wiping a few tables before joining him to help him get settled.

Buff and Faith cut out about 3:00, leaving me to finish prep for the evening meal of baron of beef sliced and served over rice with gravy and a salad. Except for hand slicing the beef into portion sizes, the whole meal was a slam dunk.

We were running well into the black these days, quite different than last year, before the fire. Mae was pressing me to take a salary increase. It of course went directly from me into the church budget in the form of tithe. We served only thirty-five regulars dinner, but four parties of travelers off the highway joined us before we closed and cleaned up.

Pastor Nate looked prepared and confident as the congregation began to arrive about 10:30 Sunday morning. Nicely dressed, with a sincere pastoral smile gracing his lips, he welcomed each as they passed through the doors into the sanctuary. Seated at the piano and playing softly, Faith had taken the first rotation as our new worship leader. Buff and the three girls were already seated in the front row smiling broadly. Although my tastes would have placed me a little farther back, Mae and I chose to join them.

As usual Tina went to Mae, calling her Nana, before handing out a big hug and kiss. The older two followed suit but with more reserve. Nate and I had not really had much alone time together over the last few weeks for personal discussion. I imagined that he had been consumed with organizing and acclimating to his new life. I watched as the church filled, with the people came a sense of ownership, of community, a gladness to meet and fellowship with one another. We had needed this new chapter in our lives for some time.

Pastor Nate stood at the lectern, joining us in several hymns before speaking. "Welcome, welcome to all. I am so pleased that God has brought us back together today to worship Him." Amens, several rang out.

"As some may have noticed, I have brought my home with me. It is parked out behind the church. If any should have need please feel free to seek me either here or there any time. I assume that many here today have known the Lord Jesus for years, others maybe only a short time, and even some are likely still searching for their salvation."

"If you'll bear with me today, I'd like to share with you and possibly make a point which you may find valuable no matter where you are spiritually." Nate spoke in a grand-fatherly tone, clearly and slowly, imparting sincerity as he did. The people seemed to be settled in, quietly listening intently, as I looked around. I was impressed that his manner commanded attention.

He began to speak... "I left the other morning, my intention was to return to Helena to retrieve my little tin box house. God provided me a traveling companion needing a ride as far as Bonner's Ferry. A young man named Tim, returning home to family and looking for employment. In the course of our trip we visited and according to God's plan, his heart was drawn to hear my testimony and later to accept Jesus as his Savior." Cheers and clapping filled the church.

"Tim then elected to continue our conversation and ride to Helena with me." The congregation seemed to be hanging on his every word, waiting for another miracle.

"Tim asked me the 'why' question that so many ask God, themselves, and each other every day. The same question I recently asked God when He called my wife home. We all try and make sense of things that are beyond our understanding, while lacking the trust and faith just to accept it as God's will. I am yet to counsel many directly, having only dealt with other pastors in training and with their personal lives up to this point. And yet I know the pain we all encounter when a child is killed, when sickness takes away those we love, or when senseless death is wrought upon the upright leaving others whom we judge as sinners. We ask why? Why God does not in His great strength banish evil, why devoted ones are taken too soon, while the unsaved remain, why? I cannot answer that question, but I have one to ask you."

"Suppose that the evil, injustice, and pain we see on this earth is only 1% of the total evil that exists in our fallen world. Suppose that God is actively restraining 99% until the end of times out of His great love for us, when He will give Satan dominion for a time before conquering sin once and for all. Rather than blaming God for the 1%, should we not be praising Him daily for the 99%? Rather than asking why we are not given more, should we not be grateful for what we are given?"

The room was quiet except for the pervasive and overwhelming presence of the Holy Spirit. Pastor Nate let the pregnant question hang in the air a few seconds before motioning Faith to play the piano. She played "Just as I Am" softly as heads bowed and hearts were filled with emotion.

Nate spoke softly, "any feeling called, please come forward while we pray and receive salvation in Jesus." A nervous cough here and there were the only sounds until finally Blake and his fiancé stood and walked quietly forward, and were welcomed by the pastor.

They spoke softly for a short time before Pastor Nate introduced the "born again" couple to the congregation. It was reminiscent of introducing a bride and groom following a wedding, except that they were both the new brides of Christ.

PART SEVEN

Each day dawns with a new promise, sometimes of sunshine, other times rain. We are called to accept that we cannot change, therefore we are also called if by nothing more than common sense, to accept God's will for our lives. If you had never read God's Word, never known His voice, never been touched by His Spirit, you would still have a sense of His being, simply by looking around yourself at His creation. So-called intellectuals struggle vainly to explain God away, coming up with all manner of hypothesis and speculation filled with error.

As I look out the front window of the Widespot Café at the majesty of the surrounding mountains, the blue sky dipping behind them, the rocks and trees covering the slopes, I am always reminded of the eternal nature of God.

It was Monday morning, once again, the coffee was dripping into the carafes and the kitchen was warming as the flattop and the fryers came up to temperature. I pondered a question that many have asked themselves, why doesn't the coffee taste as good as the grounds smell?

I was still enjoying the newness of having Sundays off, without responsibility to either cook or lead worship. It felt good, but temporary, suggesting that there may be something waiting 'just around the bend' which would fill in the time I was beginning to enjoy.

Rather than joining in the Monday ritual of slicing ham, grating potatoes, and browning toast, I decided to break the mold and set up the steam cabinet with many of the same things but self-served. I did up about 5 dozen scrambled eggs, mixed with nice chunks of fried ham, chopped onions, peppers, mushrooms, and volumes of grated cheese. I sliced up the four loaves of Mae's sourdough bread with the intention of cooking French toast to order, finishing just as Mae entered.

"Morning!" came her cheery greeting as she sat at the counter with her usual paper and coffee cup. "What are we serving this morning?"

I gave her the run down on my plan for the morning meal while letting her know we'd be out of bread before lunch. She put down her cup and joined me in the kitchen, adding to the sour dough start, readying it to bake a little later. "Smells good," she said, "maybe I'll have a plate before it gets busy." She helped herself to the eggs while I browned a couple of slices of the French toast.

How Mae held her weight was a mystery to me, eating sparingly, all the while burning vast amounts of energy in her work. Maybe a heredity thing, I guessed. She had barely begun to eat when Tom joined her at the counter and handed her the mail. We duplicated her order for him adding orange juice, just as Bill Martin made it three at the counter.

Bill began his conversation with his glowing appraisal of Pastor Nate and the service the previous day. We all agreed with nods as he continued to say that he was spreading the word up and down the corridor in his county, inviting folks to come to a service. I could tell that Mae was enjoying his endorsement of her "dear friend."

Just after 7:00 a group of students, accompanied by their coaches from the local high school, entered and were seated, helping themselves to the eggs while waiting on the French toast. Mae poured several pitchers of OJ and milk before the crowd was appeased.

The head coach had apparently arranged a service project for some of his "jocks," cleaning up and painting and maintenance at a local retirement housing community a few miles to the north. Everyone seemed in good spirits, feeling blessed to cut classes for the day with the admin's knowledge, as they boarded the bus with full stomachs.

Buff and Faith joined us just as a crew from the state highway maintenance dropped in. They were going to chip seal Highway 95 in preparation for the fall rain and winter snow. The rougher surface gave motorists much better traction while extending the overall life of the blacktop. We were told our particular section of highway would only be affected for a couple of hours, beginning early afternoon.

When the regulars began to show up it looked like the eggs were such a hit that we may run out before everyone was fed, over half of them going to the football team earlier. Buff and I supplemented them with an additional six dozen but could do nothing about the limited supply of toast.

Mae already had put several more loaves in to bake for lunch and dinner. Tom and Hazel Turner, with their children, stopped in to dine with us on their way to Radium Hot Springs in B.C. on their vacation. Tom mentioned that they had already spoken to Pastor Nate about leading a children's Sunday school class. It seemed the more I got to know them, the more I liked and respected them.

That reminded me that we had not seen Nate this morning, but did not mention it to Mae, who I was sure had already taken note. I missed having him stay in the cabin where his presence had so quickly become a part of my day.

"Morning, welcome to the Widespot," I said in my usual manner as a man and his wife sat down at the counter rather than taking a table or booth. "Coffee?" I asked, turning over their cups but waiting for reply. They nodded, and took the offered menus without speaking.

I pointed to the eggs before explaining the breakfast special which seemed not to catch their interest. "Biscuits and gravy, side of bacon, split it on two plates," the man said for both of them. I made no further attempt to engage them as I returned to prepare their order.

Mae was clearing up from the initial crowd, helping Buff buss tables, while refilling drinks. I noted that she was not limping and had not even brought her cane with her this morning. *Praise God.* Finally, about 10:30 Nate pulled up out front in his Silverado and joined the crowd inside.

"Sleeping late preacher?" I asked in my usual manner. That new job wearing on you already or the bed in the trailer not so comfortable?"

Nate smiled at me and then took a seat beside the couple at the counter before responding. "Love the job, but yes, the bed is not like being at home," he replied.

Mae took her cue, pouring him coffee and plating him some eggs without asking. "Do you want cakes or French toast?"

"Maybe just one toast," he answered with a smile. By the time he had finished his breakfast the room had cleared and Mae was sipping coffee with him at the counter. Buff, Faith and I finished up the eggs and left over French toast together at a table, while watching the front door.

"Did we hear that Tom and Hazel are going to lead Sunday school for the children?" I asked Nate.

"I hope so," he answered. "They have offered and I have accepted for the church."

I turned to Faith and Buff, "have you thought about the girls attending?"

"We haven't discussed it," they said together laughing. "We just heard today when you did."

Then Pastor Nate addressed them, "we'll be having sign-ups next Sunday and are looking for another couple to help and back them up," he said. They nodded but did not reply. I supposed that they had not come to see themselves as a couple quite yet.

"Any ideas for lunch, Buff?" I asked offhandedly, "I'm plumb out."

"How much of that 'water added' do we have left?" he asked before continuing. "Maybe grilled ham and cheese with pickles and fries."

I liked the idea, use up the ham, make it easy and simple. "Let's go with that," I said. "I think I have enough boned chicken to whip up a noodle soup for those who'd like a combo." I began cutting fries, with

Buff slicing ham thin on the slicer. Mae and Faith readied the tables for the upcoming lunch crowd.

To our surprise Sadie Hawkins, Beth, was our first lunch guest, taking the special without the ham and fries, just grilled cheese and chicken soup. Nate lingered at the counter greeting people as they came in, while sipping coffee. Mae's bread had cooled to the point of slicing just in time to feel the touch of Buffy's electric knife. Tom and Pam stopped in and shared lunch together while their daughters were in school, sitting at the counter by the new pastor.

Faith brought them cokes while I turned their sandwiches, then asked, "are the twins going to attend Sunday school? Tom and Hazel are leading it." I smiled, as did Nate, watching the grapevine spread the news. I'd bet my meager paycheck that anyone in the valley with primary school kids would be aware of the classes before next Sunday.

The highway crew joined us, some with lunch boxes of their own, some expecting to buy theirs, as they took the corner booth. The proximity to the job probably being the reason for the blessing of their business, I still felt grateful for every meal I served.

Have I told you about Mae's house? It lies adjacent to, but not on, the same property as the Widespot. She and Jib apparently bought them from the same owner but with separate deeds. Probably built post war, in early to mid-fifties, it is a wood frame house, two stories with a single detached garage sitting off to the side.

The fence between the two properties had been taken or fallen down years ago. I'd only been inside upon a few occasions, once when she had the stroke and a few times while we were keeping an eye on her during rehab. Kitchen, bath, single bedroom, and eating area on the first floor, I have never had need to venture up the steep stairway to the second.

Jib added a porch after they moved in, did the work himself, where they and now she, sits during the nice evenings. Their property backs up on Buffy's fishing stream with timber and natural grasses making it a haven for small mountain creatures and birds. She keeps her little Subaru in the garage, driving it infrequently. Jib's old Ford pickup is parked here behind the café.

Two of the men on the highway crew lived locally and were sometime visitors to the church, the others were strangers to me but also likely lived nearby as well. Old shy Nate walked right up to their table and introduced himself, they all being strangers to him. When asked to sit with them, he did, continuing to visit before inviting them to visit the church.

He was no "hard sell" kind of a salesman, but proud of his product and unabashed at presenting it. He had already actually had business cards printed and he was generous with them among the remaining patrons. Jib used to call it "planting seed," then he'd quote the story Jesus told of the seed that fell upon the hard ground, laughing his deep rich laugh. "Thing is," he'd say, "Never know what the ground is like until you plant." Yeah, I do miss Jib.

Al had delivered us three spiral cut bone-in hams, I stuck two in the oven to heat and began peeling spuds for scalloped potatoes. Next I did a garden salad with fresh spinach, lettuce, frozen peas, bean sprouts, cherry tomatoes, broccoli, green onions, and hand roasted walnut halves and sunflower seeds caramelized in cinnamon butter. Some of our red raspberries had gone over the hill so I used them to make a raspberry vinaigrette of my own creation. Buff had made a cherry cobbler that was in baking before he and Faith left for home. Mae had the condiments filled, tables wiped, and sat visiting with Nate in the empty dining room.

I joined them, holding out her usual iced tea and offering him mine before saying, "you're kind of shy Nate, don't know how you are gonna meet folks unless you come out of your shell."

We shared a laugh, then Nate replied, "we had 75 at service Sunday, not counting the kids. I'd love to have an even hundred.

I nodded, sharing his enthusiasm, then said, "that's encouraging but the only numbers that really count are the two who found Jesus. I seem to remember something about the ninety and nine and the one lost sheep."

"Not bad," he said, "how'd you like to be a deacon?"

"Got my hands full," I answered, "but I promise to think it over. I'm glad to help out but I'm not much on official titles as you can tell by my nick name."

It was just Mae and I for the dinner hour, with the new dishwasher learning to buss tables and Nate donning an apron to help with the serving. Buffy and Faith had a night off to be with their girls. Buck and family were the first in, followed closely by Glen and his own family. They pulled together three fours in the overflow, filling them right up. I enjoyed knowing that the hardship of the fire had brought them back together. Unfortunately, however, I was not to get off easy by serving them baked ham. Buck was back on his normal beef only diet and encouraged everyone at the table likewise.

Off a hanging half I cut the entire rib roast before breaking it down into 10 nice steaks, rib in. While Nate plated ham, potatoes, and salad for the other guests, I seasoned and fried six nearly raw and four medium rare before adding the potatoes and salad. I made a note to ask Buck to give me a heads up the nights they planned to arrive hungry, with guests. He apparently had no idea of what happened to the beef after it came in the back door and was hung in the cooler that turned it into dinner.

Nate was a Godsend, literally, and I told him so in the same breath that I agreed to deacon for him. It seemed every time we were getting even, another family would join us, but eventually the tables began to empty without replacements eager to take the seats. At 6:30, while Buck and company were lingering over coffee and Buff's cobbler, we served our last customer and turned the sign.

A single graced the door just as I was ready to turn away, my friend Trent Davis. He had been at some sort of meeting in Spokane and drove the two hours north just to visit. Everyone there, except Nate, had come to know and like him. He was greeted with enthusiasm and love.

"This is my friend and our new pastor Nate Walker," I said, turning from Trent toward Nate. I continued with a flourish, "and Nate, this is a witness to the great and awesome power of the Lord, Trent Davis."

I left them to visit while I filled a plate for Trent, then joined Buck and his group at their table. Tired but happy, I bricked the grill, filtered the grease from the fryer, and prepared to close up shop as the last of them left for home. It was 7:30, Mae and Nate remained finishing up bussing tables while the last of the dishes disappeared into the machine.

The remainder of the week followed the normal routine without anything significant happening until Friday night. A group of about two dozen jocks from the football team, led by Blake and the four Spellman boys, came in about 6:00. Mae, Nate, Buffy, Faith and myself were feeding the multitudes that already occupied most of the seats.

Mae yelled at me, when I turned around and looked out, it seemed the four horses of the apocalypse had arrived, times six. I left the kitchen to Buff and went to speak to the boys. Assuming they had come to eat, I tried to explain that it would be a while before they could be seated.

Blake and Thomas seemed to take the lead, "no thanks, we didn't come to eat this time, we came to see if Pastor Nate or someone could use some help, Coach sentenced us to community service rather than running laps." I almost laughed knowing we had enough horsepower right here to move a barn.

"Pastor Nate!" I called. "There are some young men here looking to serve the Lord." Nearly everyone in the room turned their heads to see what was going on.

Nate asked the boys outside where they could visit privately, restoring the oxygen to the room. "Good bunch of boys," he said as he came in the front door, "smart Coach too, I need to meet him."

The remaining customers strained to pick up the conversation, including the two from the road crew who lived nearby. "We've scheduled our first 'work party' for tomorrow morning, going to start by sweeping and cleaning up the church parking lot. Maybe next week we can get together a list of folks who need help but can't do it themselves or afford to pay to get it done."

One of the men from the highway crew came to where Nate and I were talking. "We haven't loaded the sweeper yet; it's parked almost across from the church, waiting until Monday to be hauled south. I could clear it with my boss if you like and give the lot a good power sweeping. Nate expressed his gratitude as the man got on his cell.

In a few minutes he was back, he gave us the okay and offered a couple of gallons of left over striping paint if needed. He stuck out his hand, "the name's Frank, Frank Williams. I am pleased to meet you in person. The wife and I enjoyed your sermon Sunday. We are new to the area and don't know a lot of folks yet."

We all met Frank, and Nate accepted his offer, promising to meet him here in the morning. Nate smiled broadly, "God doth provide," he said shaking his head at the manner and method of the provision.

At 6:30 when I arrived and began opening up, cars were already pulling into the lot. Nate was out front parking the boys out of the way. Like most teens, they came in ones or twos, giving us a half lot full of cars. When Frank pulled in they all came inside together and sat waiting Nate's instruction. By that time it was nearly 7:00 and I had the kitchen up to speed, having mixed up copious amounts of pancake batter, before taking the spiral sliced ham off the bone to fry.

I didn't wait for them, speaking first, "the Widespot is furnishing breakfast; pancakes and ham, coffee, milk or coffee. I am alone so I'm going need a few of you to help out."

Tom and Blake took over like team captains will, assigning each a job as I began to put a nice burn on the whole ham. It took the whole grill and messed it up bad with the sugar in the cure, but smelled wonderful. The ham in a warmer, I began pouring pancakes on the flattop, two dozen at a time. Blake joined me in the kitchen while others set silver on the tables and poured drinks. Nate and Frank watched smiling.

By the time I had poured the last, the first was ready to turn, by the time they were turned, the first were coming off three to a plate with a nice piece of ham. By the time they began pushing back from the tables, I had cooked 10 dozen pancakes and there was not a piece of ham left for Buffy or I.

Counting the two men, the work party numbered 26. The church was two miles down from the café, many of the boys elected to jog rather than drive and try and find a place to park off the lot. Others piled into the back of Nate's pickup, sagging the springs until the trailer hitch was in danger of dragging.

Buff, Mae, and Faith came in together, surveying the mess and shaking their heads before bussing the tables.

"Mae, the Widespot bought the work crew breakfast, I hope that was alright," I said with a grin. "Oh, and Mae, we are out of ham."

The day had started early and on a good note, but left me feeling behind and out of routine as I tried to get organized. The hash brown potatoes were ready to be grilled when I began to break eggs into a bowl and fry ahead several orders of sausage. Buff came by and grabbed one off the grill with a smile and kept walking.

"What's the lunch special?" he asked.

"Not a clue," I answered, "I haven't had a minute to think of one. Let's just work off the menus for breakfast and lunch and worry about a dinner special.

I called Al while I was thinking about it and added ham to my order. "Turkey?" Al asked. "How do you feel about some big birds? I can get them out at 59¢ per pound as a special."

Thinking ahead, I asked "fresh or frozen?" Frozen was the reply, making it not a dinner special, at least for today. "We'll take four, and two prime ribs for tonight's meal, make sure and grab nice ones.

"Always do," Al answered, and I knew he did. He had made his reputation selling the same quality he ate.

By the time Tom and Bill Martin came through the door together laughing, no one would have known we'd already fed the multitudes. Buff had the washer going, the tables were clean and the girls were talking quietly over coffee.

"Bill," I asked, "you are early for your usual, is this the morning you are going to broaden your horizons?"

He smiled, "I was called out early by Sadie Hawkins to investigate a gang fight in progress or vandalism at the church. She was unclear of which to report. Did you know that she lives just up the hill from the church?"

I admitted that I did not, and had never wondered either.

"Well, she does, and she was awakened this morning before eight by a street sweeper and a gang of thugs running around the parking lot." I joined him and Tom in their merriment. "I can't wait to hear her story at lunch," Mae said, having overheard.

Well, breakfast went well, everyone of course wanting ham this particular morning and grumbling because we were out, but accepting sausage as a default. About 9:00 Tom, Jean and their kids stopped and had breakfast with us on their way home from a too short vacation.

Tom bragged that they had 'churched' on Sunday with Mark, Becky and their two sons in Canmore, Alberta, who had also sent their blessings and prayers to us. I hand pressed three dozen fresh patties in preparation for lunch before running out of fresh ground beef. I was forced to take a couple of boxes of 3:1's out of the freezer.

When I called back I missed Al, who was making deliveries today himself, his son away on some work crew, his wife told me. I added 40 pounds of fresh ground for his next delivery on Monday. When Buff asked where he could help I pointed him to the potatoes that needed washing and wrapping in preparation for baking later. Mae had not been inclined to bake Parker house, so we planned to settle for brown and serve with our prime, bakers, and a veggie at $10.95.

When Al arrived, I seasoned the meat and put it right into the oven to bake at low temperature, then began helping Buff cook for the noon crowd. "Testing our patience" were the words Buffy used to describe the mess the Lord used when a water line to the dishwasher broke at the height of our lunch hour. We worked through the water, using squeegees to push most of it into floor drains, while slipping and sliding on the floor in front of the fryers and grill. I struggled, but held on to my good mood through resolve, and with Buffy's encouragement.

Most of the customers were gone when Nate, Frank, and the crew returned from their labors; hot, hungry, and in good spirits. Buff was on the grill, moving with the grace of a practiced pianist, while I topped the burgers for him and pulled the fries from the fryer.

When Sadie came in, viewed the crowd, then turned and left, we all laughed until our sides hurt. Nate told me that Frank had not only swept the lot but also overseen the layout and chalk lining of it. That allowed the boys to paint the stripes on it with 4" rollers on long handles. Several of the boys bore evidence of their labors on their person.

Frank, Nate told me, had volunteered to lead the boys youth group and hoped his wife might feel called to do the same with the girls. They had already scheduled next Saturday's project. It was to put up a pair of goal posts in the field next door. Nate and Frank split the lunch tab that I would guess was adjusted a little by Mae.

It had been a copper sweat joint that had failed, causing our flood. The fix itself was easy, but draining the line so that it could be re-soldered had proved to take the time. Both of the prime ribs came out of the oven early, being then replaced by the baked potatoes. Our intention was to serve the roast beef for supper with any left over to become our French dip at lunch on Monday.

About 3:00 I looked up when I heard the whine of a siren, just in time to see Tom's cruiser heading south at high speed. We heard later that a couple in a hurry had tried to pass on a double line and met a farm tractor on a curve. Ted Adams, a local, and the couple traveling through were all killed instantly. Ted was one of those who had helped Glen set up the wheel line on Buck's property during the fire. He left behind a wife and two teenagers still in middle school. Although I did not know him by name, Mae was able to describe the family who joined us occasionally to eat, well enough to recognize them.

They had been among those who had joined us at the Sunday tent service for prayer. Mae began mobilizing our little community by phone, passing the word, making arrangements to deliver food and support even before calling the Adams' home. In the five years I had made my home in this little valley, this was only the second death I was aware of, Faith's husband being the other.

When the dinner hour came, we were over-flowing with guests, most however were subdued and more concerned with discussing the bad news than with food. Mae's fish bowl was nearly full of contributions by the time we turned the sign and began our cleanup.

What I was to find out, and was already evident to most; a rancher or farmer is a self-employed businessman, depending nearly 100% on the owner for its income. Unlike Buck, whose children were of age to take over, disability or death was often the final straw leading to bankruptcy and then homelessness. Seldom was there enough income to both feed the family and hire outside help. Occasionally, if the real estate was owned rather than mortgaged, the land could be leased out, providing sustenance at a minimal level.

About 7:30 Mae finally called, having delayed to give others closer to the family first chance to make contact. Nate took the phone when offered it, giving his own condolences before offering to call on them at a later, more appropriate time. After he hung up, the three of us took turns praying together for Avis and the family for strength, mercy, and healing.

Bake sales and all manner of fundraisers and charity benefits were born out of need in the early American small communities, long before insurance became an answer to the mortality of mankind. Since man cannot replace those whom God has called home, he always turns to the small part which he can replace, the financial loss.

When we arrived at the church, many were already there discussing and sharing information concerning the tragedy of the previous day. Avis and her children were not in attendance, but more than a hundred were. Buck and Glen were huddled with a couple of others, deep in discussion in one corner of the sanctuary. When Faith's replacement began to play the piano, most found seats and began to sing along as Nate lead them in 'How Great Thou Art'.

After the second hymn, Pastor Nate recounted what he had been told of Ted's death and the death of the other couple, then he knelt and invited any who would, to join him before he began praying. It was a difficult time for many who were suffering loss of a friend, but also a chance for God to strengthen the faith of the community.

Nate went right to his sermon, not the one he had labored to prepare during the week, but the one God had put in his heart just last night. Nate spoke with passion about the uncertainty of life on earth, about the certainty of God's promises, about the danger of waiting to make spiritual commitment, and about the grace and mercy our loving God held for each of His children.

Some of what he needed to say would not have been appropriate if Avis and the children were present, their wounds too fresh. For the rest of us, it was a wake up call that some still needed to hear. Nate did not hold an open altar call, but encouraged any who sought the Lord to see him privately after the service.

We joined in worship a final time before Nate shared the more welcome news that affected the church. He told us of the youth group's project, it's new leadership, and his personal commitment to support them both personally and financially. Just as it seemed that he may be finished, Mae stood and asked for the floor.

Nate invited her to the front where she brought the attendees up to speed regarding what she knew of the needs of the Adams family. The fishbowl already held several hundred dollars and stood ready to accept additional donations from the community.

Mae was coordinating food donations and would have a better handle on how others may help once she had been out to see the family. She took several questions from the floor and accepted information from friends in the know. At this point we had no idea of where, when, or who might hold the funeral or if there was a need to help with accommodations for out-of-town guests. Nate promised to be the 'clearing house' for information as it came in.

Glen spoke next, although he had some trouble because of his emotion, letting the congregation know the condition of the crops in the fields. Additionally, where needs may lie for help as the crops matured and were harvested before being marketed. He asked any with equipment and knowledge to contact him directly to coordinate their efforts rather than Avis.

We realized that the timing of the tragedy could have been much worse had it been earlier in the season. When the service closed most did not leave immediately, rather they gathered in groups to discuss and formulate plans to help the family.

Mae and Glen's wife Maureen made plans to take out food together in the afternoon. Once back at the Widespot Mae, Nate, and I began putting roast beef sandwiches together for later delivery while Buffy made a nice salad and some brownies for dessert. After Mae and Nate had gone to pick up Maureen, Buff confided in me some good news. Faith was nearly two months pregnant. Words from an old song came to mind, "He gives and takes away."

I heard Mae's car drive into her driveway after 10:00 but didn't go out to see her. I supposed that emotion, coupled with the long day, probably made her needing a bed more than a guest. I did not sleep well, instead I spent a good deal of the night trying in vain to understand the workings of God's mind. We were all back to asking the "why" question that Nate had answered so well only a week before. While this seemed a 'bad' thing, a terrible thing for his family, was it really? How much worse could it have been?

Then a thought came into my mind, what if he had not been killed but only paralyzed, what if the crops were yet to be planted? What if the children had been babies or his wife was ill? But, most of all, what if he had never known Jesus as his Savior?

It did help a little, and as I drifted off to sleep, I thought of how we often blame God for not preventing bad things from happening, but seldom thank Him for the many He does prevent. I felt loss, loss for a man I had never known, or hardly known. Oddly, it seemed that something, not someone, had been lost from my world making it somehow less than it had been. I wondered if when Faith's child were born I'd have a sense of balance again.

When I awoke, there was a song on my lips, or in my head if you prefer, arriving there without my effort or encouragement. The words played over and over as I showered, the message making it's point.

Turn on the lights, the vent fan, light up the grill and the fryers, start the coffee, check stock, formulate a plan for the day. The routine of the day played as if an old movie on a continuous loop, my movements mechanical and uninspired. I found myself without vitality and feeling hopeless and depressed.

A thought entered my mind, "is this all there is to life?" As the enemy, Satan, fought to get a foothold in my life, the Righteous Brothers' song flooded back, "you are my hope and highest inspiration..." They sang of a person, I thought of Jesus.

By the time Mae arrived, leaning on her cane for the first time in weeks, I was rockin' out to my CD with Bill Medley's bass voice providing my encouragement. Mae smiled as she 'coffee'd up' and sat down with her paper.

"How are Avis and the kids?" I asked, turning down the tunes.

"She's a strong woman," she offered. "The kind of frontier woman who came across the country and helped settle it, who buried husbands and children along the way. They have family coming in from Grangeville, somewhere in Colorado, and a few from back east. Avis hopes to have the funeral Friday or Saturday if they all arrive. I told her we had four cabins available as she might need them. She asked Nate if he'd do the service. I 'spect that she'll be contacting the funeral home today to make the arrangements."

Don Taylor entered with the day's mail and the look of a man who needed company. "Don," I said, inclining my head, "coffee?"

He nodded, "am I too early for some eggs and toast?"

"Never," I answered, "how do you want them?"

"How about over easy for a change so I can sop up the yolk with the toast like my Dad used to do?"

"You got it," I answered, turning to the grill. Don sat next to Mae and discussed the uncertainty of life made abundantly clear to all of us by Ted's death.

"My wife didn't want me to go to work today," he said. "This thing with Ted really got to her. Our kids have gone to school together and played sports since grade school. We had lunch together Sunday after church."

Mae nodded, then said, "we all have been touched by this, many more than they realize now. I'll give Nell a call a little later, maybe we can visit."

Don thanked her and broke the yolk on his eggs, smiling up at me. "Just right," he said.

Buffy and Faith came in, both looking younger than I felt, a kind of glow about them. I surmised it had something to do with their excitement over their pregnancy. When Buff came back wrapping an apron around himself, I noticed he had lost some weight, so I commented. "Looks like that apron is getting too big for you, Buff."

He smiled and said, "I have been trying to lose a few pounds, I'm down seven since the first of the month, twelve overall."

"That's great, it shows, keep up the good work," I encouraged.

Finally, I had had enough of soul and inspiration so I turned off the CD player, but was feeling better about what the day might provide. I said a silent prayer of thanks and one for Don and Nell and their family.

Tom DeGrange and Bill came in together this particular morning, their cars parked side by side near the door. Neither man looked himself and although I attempted to draw them out in conversation, both seemed to be carrying the burdens of their job. I did not doubt that both had been on the scene and bore witness to the carnage that continued to tear at their hearts.

I poured coffee for both while Faith and Mae were visiting in the corner booth and then offered breakfast. Neither man seemed excited about eating, Tom ordered only a short stack with one egg and Bill an English muffin with Mae's jam as they continued to visit quietly.

Nate came in, greeted the room, then sat by Bill and Tom, who had just gotten their meals. They were blessing them privately with closed eyes and bowed heads. I watched as Nate sipped his coffee quietly, observing them out of the corner of his eye but not joining them in conversation.

Finally, he leaned toward them as their conversation lulled and said quietly, "we are going to have a quiet time Wednesday evening at the church, around 7:00, for folks to gather, talk, cry, and try to make sense of this thing that has happened. It'd be good for children to be included too, they are likely feeling insecure and worried about the uncertainty of their own futures."

What I observed in their eyes was amazing, hope... hope that there might be an answer to some of their own questions. In just a few words Pastor Nate had restored hope in them.

I found this man, whom I hardly knew, had the God-given ability to instill hope and give comfort to others. He continued to stay and visit privately with those who came for breakfast and then lunch. He would join them right where they sat, offering his short message of encouragement before moving on. I found it ironic that he had never lead a congregation before, and yet had quickly become so well attuned to it's needs. I noticed when Tom and Bill left they walked with purpose once again, even laughing and talking as they went out the door together.

Family after family of regulars came and went, each receiving the same invitation, each being touched individually by it. Following breakfast, I prepared for lunch as always with Buffy helping, while Faith and Mae readied the dining area.

Between the sandwiches Mae had taken to the Adams farm and the dinners we had served on Saturday, little had remained of the prime rib roasts to serve as French dip today. Finally, when Faith and Mae were ready, they came together to share the good news with me. I looked at Buff but said nothing, pretending to share their excitement as I had with Buffy earlier. I could see that he was grateful for keeping his secret.

Whenever we lacked the stamina to be creative and determine a special of the day, we resorted to the regular menu as we did today. I always felt slightly guilty, as though I had somehow cut corners for our guests. About 2:00, Nate took his leave saying he had matters to attend to, but promising to dine with us at the evening meal.

Fresh rolls were in the ovens, potatoes boiling for garlic mashed, and three dozen thick cut pork chops had been opened with a knife and stuffed with dressing. They would replace the rolls in the oven about 3:30 where they would bake, then be kept warm for dinner. Buffy had made a nice pork gravy which simmered on the side burner and a green salad.

Our first dinner guests dropped in about 4:30, a couple from Pasco, Washington on their way to Canada. Mae seated them at a table and explained our special while pouring their drinks. Members of the community joined us, many in the same reserved, subdued manner that Tom and Bill had brought with them earlier in the morning.

When Nate joined us, he began the same routine as he had before, and with much the same effect. Several commented that they had already heard his message of encouragement from others and planned to be there Wednesday evening. I could tell that they had come together to draw strength from one another. After we had closed and cleaned up Monday evening, the five of us stayed on a while longer, talking and discussing the events of the past few days.

Tuesday was a duplicate of Monday in the sense that many sought the Widespot as a place to gather and find solace with one another. Wednesday morning, Mae beat me to the kitchen. The coffee was already on, and two sheet cakes were in the oven when I came in. Once again the cane had been left home and her vitality seemed to have returned. She showed me her left hand, giving me a million dollar smile, where her wedding set had been replaced by an engagement ring.

"Nate asked me to marry him," she offered. "We had planned to wait, until the accident made it clear that we should not delay in accepting God's gift of second love." I offered her my sincere congratulations, feeling a little contrite in the fact that I had seen it from the day they had met. Another testimony of the faithfulness of God and for His provision for each of us.

Right then, in the middle of things, Satan loosed an arrow which stuck, burning in my shield... one strange and unfamiliar to me. Where is that someone created just for Bum Roberts, the one God created to fulfill and complete me? Funny thing, until that moment I had never ever pictured myself married or with a wife and children. Self analysis often leads one astray, but here my intuition was telling me that I too had felt the sting of loss from Ted's death, only in a different way than most. Some describe it as 'the edge of your faith,' the place where doubt tries to creep in. Will there be someone for me, I wondered?

Mae and I rode together to the church early so that she could arrange the cake and refreshments with other women of the congregation. Nate accepted my congratulations warmly before being interrupted by a continuing flow of guests who sought his attention. The sanctuary was nearly full at about ten when Avis and the children arrived with Glen and his family. The room got very quiet for a few moments until she set them at ease by making a little joke about nearly being late... she stopped before saying what was in everyone's minds... for your own funeral.

Nate began by thanking everyone for coming, emphasizing that this was a very informal affair, at which anyone should feel free to speak and express their feelings without reservation. He acknowledged that emotions were likely to effect what and how we heard others and preached care in making judgments. He opened us in prayer, asking for healing, mercy, and grace, then for strength to endure and overcome.

He acknowledged God's plan and unknowable ways that left us crying out for answers to our questions. Then He closed by thanking God for His love that provided a way for us to live and know each other in the life yet to come. Several cried softly including Avis and the children. Nate finally stopped talking and said, "any who might like to express how they feel please do."

Mae stood, to my surprise, and began to speak. "You know me," she said, "and most of you knew Jib, my husband. I remember when he died, I thought I had died too, the pain was so deep and harsh. But God had known of my need long ago and had brought a friend into our lives well in advance to help me through the pain, Bum Roberts. He has walked with me, prayed with me, and been the strong right hand of God in my sorrow. God does provide."

She sat and another took her place, then another, and another. Everyone cried, then laughed, then cried again. Finally Don Taylor stood and spoke, then Nell, and finally their children with tears running down their cheeks, gasping to form words through their pain and fear. The Adams' children embraced them, holding onto them like anchors, rocking back and forth sharing the pain of loss. Time flew by, finally we were emotionally spent and laughter began to replace the tears, many told jokes on themselves involving Ted or the family, times and memories shared.

When Nate resumed the podium, he closed by reminding us that Jesus had been called 'a man of sorrows', that our sin had allowed sorrow to enter God's creation and bruise and wound us, but never to be allowed to kill us. Jesus is the promise of eternal life and holds the promise of the end of all sorrow. He prayed with us, then invited us to go downstairs and enjoy some refreshments. I doubt that there was anyone who was not famished and dehydrated by the two hours of cleansing we had just endured. It was 9:00 when I left, leaving Nate to bring Mae home, and the party was still underway.

PART EIGHT

"Good morning, welcome," I said to the newcomer who had been first in the door Thursday. "Coffee?" I poured her a cup, then slid a menu across the counter to where she sat. "I'm John Roberts, locals call me Bum." She did look up when I said Bum but did not speak, looking at the right hand side of the menu. I take notice of things like that, having been on the road myself and watching my budget.

She drank down both the water and the coffee and let me pour another before she spoke. "How much for the ham and eggs without the hash browns?" she asked.

"Same price," I answered, "but, if you don't like my hash browns, you can substitute something else if you'd like." She went back again to the right side obvious in her attempt to get the most for her money.

"But, I'll tell you what, being the first customer of the day gives your meal for free anyway... order as you like." She looked at me critically, "free? Yeah right, nothing is free, what's your gimmick?"

No gimmick," I said, "I'll get the ham started while you decide how you'd like your eggs and if you want to try my homemade hash browns." I returned to the kitchen and put a nice piece of bone-in on the flattop as Buffy came through the rear door.

"Morning Buff," I said casually, "how did things go last night?"

"Stayed until almost 10:00," he said, "folks just wanted to visit and share their feelings."

I leaned through the window looking at our guest, "how do you like your eggs?" I asked.

"Over hard and break the yolks," she answered, smiling this time, "and scatter the spuds, well done."

"You got it," I answered, "white or wheat?"

"Wheat, and thank you."

Mae came in smiling, carrying her paper, poured a cup and took a chair beside the woman.

I hurried to cover my tracks, "good morning, Mae," I said. "This young woman is the first guest of the day, winner of the free breakfast."

Mae did not even blink, "well congratulations, I hope Bum does us proud. You got any complaints, come see me, name's Mae," she said holding out her hand.

"Bonnie," the woman said, returning the smile and shaking her hand, "and thank you, I will."

"Mae," Buffy said through the window, "Faith may be late or not at all, got the morning sickness."

"We'll make do," Mae answered him, "she pretty bad?"

"Well, I don't know much about these things," Buff admitted, "but I never did see her, just heard her while I was getting the kids off to school."

Mae smiled again as I delivered Bonnie's breakfast. "Ham, two well done, spuds scattered and whole wheat, want juice?"

Bonnie gave me a smile, "orange juice if it's no trouble," she answered, "sorry I gave you a hard time. I'm on the road alone, hard to get used to folks not trying to get you alone in a corner."

It was my turn to smile, "that's how I came by my name, on the road alone looking for my place in the world. They thought I looked the part here when I showed up."

She was mostly blond, some streaks of a darker color bleached by the sun, about five and a half feet, maybe 110-115, looked pretty fit. If I were guessing, she might be about my age or a little younger, was hard to tell. Her nose and face were covered with freckles, with deep set blue eyes and what might have been dimples if she gained a pound or two.

"Hitching or walking?" I asked.

"Neither," she replied, "riding a bike mostly, carrying it right now with a second flat tire." Outside, nearly out of sight, was a good quality bike with gear bags across the rear fender, both tires flat.

I turned to Buff. "Buffy, do we still have that patch kit somewhere for bike tires?"

"Yeah," he answered, "I think it's out in one of the cabins, not sure which one."

"I tell you what, Bonnie, if we can make it through the breakfast rush, maybe we can find the patch kit and get you back on the road," I volunteered. She did not answer, but smiled and continued eating her breakfast.

When they did come, they came without dragging despair along behind them on a chain. Although the pain of loss was still fresh among them, they had begun to heal, the wound had already began to scab over.

Don Taylor, Bill, Tom, and even Al enjoyed breakfast with us. Buck and his entourage came and knocked out several pounds of bacon before pushing back from their table. When it became evident that Mae was struggling to keep up, Buff began bussing tables, but was sent back into the kitchen to help me by Bonnie, who jumped right in.

One could tell that she was no stranger to work and had also waited tables before. It proved to be one of our biggest breakfasts ever in numbers served, almost every face from last night came through the front door hungry and wanting to talk. Thank God, they were spaced over several hours and never quite over-turned the boat.

As the last group left the Widespot laughing, arms around each other, headed off in separate directions, we four sat at one of the dirty tables enjoying the moment. Sweaty and tired, we reveled in our victory together as we drank our iced drinks and relived the experience.

It felt like Bonnie had been with us forever, rather than someone off the street four hours earlier, who still did not have a last name. It was Mae who said, "Bonnie, you may have to be careful. This is just how Bum started and is still here after six years." We all laughed.

Buff and I retired to the kitchen to get things in order and prepare for lunch, while Mae and Bonnie wiped, bussed, and refilled in the dining area. It was 11:00 by the time we finished and the first of the hungry lunch hoards breached the draw bridge.

Neither Mae nor Bonnie sat down over the next three hours, pausing only briefly to deliver an order, refill a drink, or buss a table. Buff and I had found our groove and kept up well, serving our 'hot and fresh' time after time. Nate came and went, eating and visiting with guests.

We had no time to talk with him except to find out that the funeral was set for Saturday at 2:00. Mae posted a hastily written note on the register to help pass the word along as people came and went. When they quit coming, it was like someone shut off the faucet, with no stragglers or late comers at all.

Buff was at the dishwasher since our college boy was back in school now and only worked weekends. I surveyed the cooler and settled upon another 'chicken fried steak' special, since none of the rounds had been cut off the hanging beef yet. Six full cut rounds yielded about 15 pounds of meat, that when cubed, should feed 30-40 nicely. I put salted water on to heat for the mashed potatoes and another smaller one for the gravy, then turned to creating a seasoned flour.

Buffy, who had left a few minutes before, came in the back door sporting a grin and carrying the patch kit. I started to take it from him intending to see if I could patch her tires, but he held back.

"Let me see what I can do," he said, "I've gotten pretty good at it now with the three girls and three bicycles." I deferred to his expertise, pleased at his offer.

As I was making a nice broccoli and cauliflower salad, I watched out the window as Bonnie and Buffy upended the bike and began to remove the tires. Mae had finally taken a seat but was wrapping napkins around the silverware in preparation for supper. I came out and joined her, grabbing a handful of rubber bands and napkins myself.

"Have you and Nate set a date?" I asked, "and have you discussed what effect your marriage might have on the Widespot? She looked at me with surprise evident on her face.

"No," she answered, "Ted's death has set other priorities for the moment and we haven't felt pressed to rush into it. As to the café," she continued, "I honestly hadn't given it a thought. I'm afraid I just pictured things to remain the same forever, I guess. I know that is unfair to everyone, now that I think of it, both the customers and the staff, but mostly to you.

"Mae," I said, "don't fret. God brought me here, Buffy and the others too, for His own purpose. Now He has brought Nate here as well, and not to upset the apple cart, but to serve His children. 'His timing and His plan are always perfect' Jib told me that the first day I worked here. He convinced me that my stopping here was no accident. I have since come to believe that."

Mae smiled sweetly, remembering Jib, most likely.

Buffy had come in and was using the deep sink to find the holes in the tubes, with Bonnie helping mark the holes. They found two in one and one in the second, most likely from the goat heads that thrived along the roadsides and graveled rest stops.

Bonnie carried a pump on the bike with her, enabling her to accommodate the slow leaks in the beginning and make it as far as she did. When they had patched the tubes and reassembled the tires onto the bike, they entered together laughing. "He slimed me," Bonnie accused, pointing at Buffy.

Mae and I smiled, having no clue, looked to Buff for explanation.

"I had a bottle of 'slime' with me in the car," he explained, "for our girls. It coats the inside of the tube and seals most punctures without having to take the tire off." They both joined us wrapping silverware.

Finally Bonnie said, "I best be heading out I expect, how far is the next town?"

I answered, "that depends whether you are going north or south, about 20 miles one way, 30 the other."

"Oh," she said.

Buffy joined the conversation, "a lot of it is uphill going north, mostly flat going south or downhill until you get to Lewiston."

Mae watched her reaction then said, "we have an extra cabin out back, might be well to spend the night and get an early start... no charge to you. We all appreciated your help today and Bum has a nice meal planned for supper too."

She looked at me and smiled, "I'll bet he does."

At 4:00, Bill stopped for coffee and information about the funeral to pass on. While he was still there, Mae seated a table of four from the road crew who had finished the seal coating job and were returning equipment to storage somewhere north of us. Frank was the only one I recognized from our earlier meeting.

When Buffy called home, he found that Faith was doing better but still wasn't up to caring for her energetic girls. He promised to leave as soon as the dinner hour was over and bring food with him.

Bonnie and Mae were working in harmony with each other as they had earlier, when the tables began to fill. They looked like mother and daughter out there. I noticed that somewhere along the line Bonnie had changed clothes and cleaned up since lunch. I found myself staring as she tossed her head while visiting with a customer, her short cut blond hair bouncing like an Olympian in a hair conditioner commercial.

Although most of the children wanted burgers and fries, or chicken, we served thirty-two specials, holding six back for ourselves. Nate joined us about 6:00, but waited to eat until Mae could take a break with him. Buffy left right after, with a tub of chicken, fries, and two chicken fried steak dinners. Bonnie and I served the few remaining guests while Nate and Mae took a table by themselves about 7:00.

I turned the Open sign, then sat at the counter where Bonnie had just began to eat. I blessed my food and joined her while sipping iced tea. "So Bonnie," I began, "how do you like life here at the Widespot?"

She seemed to consider what I had said before answering.

"Kind of laid back, comfortable, friendly, neighborly," she said, using a string of carefully thought-out adjectives.

"And... the people," I continued, "what is your first impression of them?"

She smiled broadly, looking me right in the eye as she repeated the four again, then added, "loving." I tried to not acknowledge that my heart had just done a flip-flop.

Then I continued, "funny, that is about how I would have described it when I came here with a pack on my back six years ago."

We finished eating but continued to talk before returning to the cleanup that remained. I filled the dishwasher with its final load and returned to the kitchen chores as Mae and Bonnie made the dining area ready for morning. Nate sat at the counter visiting with me through the serving window.

He filled me in on the funeral plans for Saturday and the reception in the church basement afterward. The church women had come together to provide the meal. He said that he expected an overflow crowd and asked if I would help him with setting up additional seating which he had rented in town. I committed to both picking up the chairs and seeing to their set up, and also returning them as well. It had become apparent that we would be closed Saturday. I reminded myself to let Buffy know and put up a sign for the public.

Rather than use a cabin, I found out that Mae had invited Bonnie to her home as a guest, using the excuse that the Adams family may need them and she wanted the company. While both were technically true, I suspected there may be more to it than just that.

It was Thursday night and, although tired, I had trouble sleeping. My mind seemed cluttered with fleeting thoughts and ideas, none lasting long enough to take shape or form ideas. I might describe it as though you were trying to grasp a strand of hair under water, just as you think you have hold if it, it disappears between your fingers.

Friday morning – fish day. A call to Al yielded fresh flash-frozen haddock reasonably priced and in abundance. I ordered 35 pounds, figuring 6 ounces per serving I could serve about 90 fish and chip dinners, then began to peel potatoes to run through the mandolin later.

As the grill and the fryers heated, I finished making a second pot of coffee, just as Mae and Bonnie entered together laughing. To my surprise, when I offered them breakfast, they both accepted. Mae seldom ate until later in the morning, and then only after her coffee and newspaper. Today, they both had two over medium, hash browns and links. That seemed like a winner also to Buffy when he joined our happy group and then Nate who followed him in. With three at the counter, I decided to make it unanimous, taking my own plate with me.

We finished eating before 7:00 when I opened officially for the day, everyone in good spirits. Bill was our first customer but before I could greet him, Bonnie made a big deal that his meal was free... on the house. She looked me right in the eye and smiled as she said it. I knew I had been caught and went right along with it.

"Yeah, Bill," I said, "a new policy here at the Widespot, the cook buys his first guest breakfast."

Neither Buffy or Nate had a clue but smiled anyway. When Tom DeGrange joined us, Bill ribbed him, "should have got up a little earlier Tom, Bum buys the first customer breakfast. Wait until I tell Don what he missed."

Now, I'd like to take a minute to remind you that lying, even white lies done for a good reason, are still a sin. Sin does have it's consequences. I had to laugh to myself when I remembered a verse somewhere that said 'be sure your sin will find you out."

Bonnie's blue eyes were dancing with mischief as she watched me react. I made a point to ring up Bill's meal and drop the money in the till while everyone watched and laughed. Bill turned to Bonnie and asked, "you just passing through or planning to stick around?"

I got the blue eyes back as she said, "well, Mae has asked me to help out for a while until Faith gets back on her feet. We'll have to wait and see how she does."

Buffy joined the conversation, "now, that's service! he said. "Faith and I were praying just this morning that God would provide while she has the morning sickness and I guess He already has."

Two travelers came in and were seated by the window, accepting coffee and menus before speaking. "We are up from Priest River for a funeral tomorrow. Can anyone tell us where it will be and if there is any place to stay?"

Mae took the reins, "the funeral is at 2:00, the church is on the highway a couple of miles south, and you just came through the only town with a motel on your way here. We have a cabin I could let you have for the night if you don't find better."

The men seemed satisfied but one asked, "what does the cabin cost?"

"Don't cost nuthin' but you could drop a donation in the fishbowl here if you like, money goes to the family to help with expenses."

Both were eating their ham and eggs when Nate joined them at their table and introduced himself. It turned out that both men had known Ted in high school years before, and had heard about the tragedy via the valley grapevine.

The breakfast crowd finally dwindled, then ceased about 10:45. I returned to prepare the fish Al had brought. They were still semi-frozen, so portioning them into serving sized chunks worked well with the aid of my heavy chef's knife. I left the fish out to soften while I prepared a pre-mix tempura batter and added my own seasonings. Buffy was chipping the potatoes using the mandolin, having already prepared coleslaw as a side.

When I felt satisfied that the fish was sufficiently defrosted, I began dipping and then precooking the chunks. My plan was to cook it all partially, set it aside, clean up the mess and the fryers and finish the cooking as needed later on with the potatoes. I had tested this method before with finger steaks to prevent all of the batter mess in the fryers during the dinner hour.

Bonnie breezed into the kitchen where we were working, "sorry about this morning," she said, "I thought I owed you one."

I couldn't help laughing at the casual way she approached life and me in particular.

"Are we about even now," I asked kiddingly, "or should I be watching over my shoulder?" She winked, smiled, then greeted our first lunch guests. I reminded Buff that we would be closed Saturday for the funeral and checked my signage to make sure it warned customers of the same.

As the wheel filled up, the fryers were busy, as was the grill. I had forgotten to make sauce so I jumped on it while Buff took over for me. A red sauce with horseradish and a tartar sauce with a twist of lemon, seasoned salt, and chopped pickles went into the portion cups. Familiar faces and names came and went as always. Most had a sense of relief about them, just seeing each other gave them a little more assurance of the permanency that they had lost in the suddenness of their friend's death.

Toward the end of the lunch hour Avis, with her children and four whom I presumed were out of town family, took a table. Mae huddled for a moment with Bonnie before allowing her to greet and take their orders. I assumed that she had been explaining their situation and who they were.

By the time I filtered the oil from the fryers, following a quick cleanup in the kitchen, it was 2:00 and I found over half of my fish already served. I sliced 20 petite sirloins from the hanging half, then reduced the fish serving proportionately before changing the special to surf and turf for the supper hour. Jib had told me to be creative.

Nate and Mae excused themselves to handle last minute details concerning the funeral service. Buffy left with food for Faith and the girls, promising to return before supper. That left Bonnie and I alone sipping iced tea at the counter.

"Bum," she asked, "tell me a little more about all of these folks I have met in the last 24 hours. Everyone seems to have a story."

"They do," I said, "I hope you have a while."

I began the now familiar story with myself and my chance meeting with Jib and Mae, I gave a thin sketch of myself leaving much of it out. Then what I knew about Jib and Mae, both before and after my arrival. Working my way down the list; Buffy, Faith, Tom, Bill, Al, Blake, Buck, Glen... and the list went on and on. Some she had met, others were yet to meet.

I found myself deeply involved in each, holding their information close to my heart, offering only the most cherished memories as I spoke about each reverently. I had to come to grips with the fact that I loved each one of them like a brother or sister, a fact that I had never taken time to consider. "God would like that," Jib said, as clearly as if he'd been with us.

About a quarter of four Nate and Mae returned with the Adams' four out-of-towners, driving back to the cabins. I assumed they had accepted the lodging that she had offered.

I turned to Bonnie, "where are you staying tonight?" I asked, immediately regretting it.

She paused as I reddened, then spoke, "why? You got somewhere in mind?"

I felt 15 again, clumsy, embarrassed, and tongue tied. I stammered to explain, only making it worse as she continued to keep a straight face and hold me in her critical stare. When she could stand it no longer she burst out in laughter.

"Bum, you are such a boy scout!" She knew and I knew from that moment that we were drawn to each other. Mae entered through the rear door smiling, giving me a sense that I had been caught with my hand in the cookie jar. Here is old Bum, just a little south of forty years old, looking and acting like a school boy.

Buffy followed whistling, not a care in the world.

"How's things?" Mae asked, referring to Faith and the kids.

"Fine as frog hair," Buff answered, laughing as if he'd told the funniest joke in the world. The Doc said the baby is fine, he gave Faith something to settle her stomach, and the girls are loving the fact they'll have a baby brother in the spring. Faith sends her thanks to Bonnie and can't wait to meet her. I caught Bonnie's smile out of the corner of my eye.

"What's for supper, Bum?" Buffy asked.

"Surf and turf," I answered. "I needed to stretch the fish out, so I added steak to the special. Do we need more coleslaw?"

Buff nodded, "I'll make a couple more gallons." I jumped onto the potatoes again, peeling, then chipping them before covering them with water.

I turned to where Mae was filling the condiments and laying out silver and asked, "are things moving along smoothly for the reception?"

"Yes, I think so," she answered. "What do you have that we could use as backup if we run short of food?"

"Quick and easy?" I asked. "How about spaghetti and meat balls?"

"I like it!, Mae said with enthusiasm.

Bonnie had been listening to our conversation, apparently with interest. "Can I help? I make a mean meatball."

Mae gave her the nod, "sure, show Bum how it's done," she said smiling.

Mae had baked four dozen Parker house rolls Thursday, most of which we still had on hand for tonight. We had A-1 and steak sauce on the tables, so I supplemented both the remaining tartar and the red sauce for the fish and declared us ready, just as the first family entered for dinner.

Jim Johnson, his wife and three children, were seated and served.

They did not come often and I did not know his wife's name or the two boys and a girl at their side. Jim runs the nearest we have to a grocery, until you get to a real town. He provides for our daily needs, much like a quick stop does in large communities.

Tom and Hazel – I almost didn't recognize Tom out of uniform – took a booth by the window, where Tom's back was against the wall with the room within his view. A frequent practice among those with law enforcement backgrounds. Sadie, as usual, was along and seated herself near them at a table.

I was surprised to see Faith and the girls come in and order just like before she and Buff were married. She looked well and hardly showed her pregnancy. The Turners, with Katy and the other children, ordered specials and burgers, striking up conversations with Glen and Maurine. They had all been close to the Adams' and were no doubt trying to give and find encouragement in their loss. Nate sat at the counter visiting with a couple unknown to me before scattering himself about the room, offering a friendly hand and smile.

Buffy and I filled the air with a fine mist of cooking oil and the scent of fresh fish and frying beef steaks. The dining area continued to fill and the earlier guests lingered over coffee and dessert, enjoying conversations and unusual fellowship. Mae opened up the overflow area where Bonnie seated and served additional hungry souls like the Green family, with their twin girls.

As soon as a table would be cleared, it seemed that their replacements would arrive, right on cue. I was just beginning to worry if we'd have enough food to accommodate the unusual numbers when Buck and company came in. They had to wait until two tables were available before they could be seated together.

I ran to the walk-in finding just enough left to cut six hardy rib steaks off a front quarter. Mae was introducing Bonnie to the crowd while they filled and refilled drinks, replaced empty plates with full ones, and offered up desserts. Nate was still working the crowd in his usual manner, offering friendship and encouragement in the Lord, while giving instruction regarding the funeral.

Buffy and I had cleaned the entire kitchen, washed all the pots and pans, processed the glass and silverware through the washer and were waiting on the last few to filter out. It was after 8:00 before the final tables were wiped and reset for Monday morning. About 9:00 I showered and fell into bed, too tired to worry about tomorrow.

I awoke at 7:00, brushed my teeth, attempted to tame my thinning hair before finally choosing a ball cap as the best cure, and went to the café. Coffee first, then lights, fans, and laying out items for the promised spaghetti.

I opened two 10 lb cans of marinara sauce, added ½ cup sweet dried basil, 2 cups chopped yellow onions, two pounds sliced mushrooms, and a ¼ cup each of sugar and salt before putting it all on to simmer. In another pot, the salted water for the noodles was heating when Bonnie and Mae entered. We exchanged greetings before the women helped themselves to coffee at the counter. They were somewhat subdued at first, also possibly feeling the strain of last night.

Finally, Bonnie called out through the window, "let me know when you have room for me to begin the meatballs."

"Come on in when you are ready and let me know what you need," I answered, curious to watch her cook. Bonnie came right in wrapping an apron around her slim waist, then went right to the sink and washed her hands. So far so good, I thought to myself.

She started asking me for things, beginning with an extra large stainless steel bowl, then the ground beef, eggs, corn meal, onion soup mix, onions, Parmesan cheese, salt, pepper, garlic, and finally olive oil. She slipped what appeared to be a class ring into her jeans, then started by breaking eggs into the bowl full of hamburger, adding full cups of corn meal, soup mix, grated cheese, and chopped onions, and the other ingredients.

It took several minutes for her to massage everything thoroughly together by hand before she deftly rolled one into a golf ball size and tossed it onto the hot grill. It cooked, with her rolling it often to brown all over, before she removed it and cleft it in half, handing me a sample. She nibbled hers, then immediately added a half cup of onion powder and remixed the entire batch. I found it quite tasty, but wouldn't have said anything had I not.

When cooked and cooled, she split the second one with Mae, who nodded her approval before speaking.

"Take some notes, Bum, she can teach you something." That of course brought a smile to Bonnie's lips and a pretend pout to my own.

I tended the little balls of meat on the flattop while she continued to roll them. It took another hour to finish the project together. We ignored several knocks on the front door by people who obviously couldn't read.

My sauce passed Bonnie's taste test so she added the meat balls to the mixture to simmer and allow the flavors to blend. When I asked Mae how she wanted to serve it, she indicated the two heated roasters that we had used for the baked spaghetti would be a perfect fit again.

After the women left to clean up and dress, I boiled and drained the spaghetti noodles before splitting them between the two pans. I added a couple more pounds of grated cheese, let it melt in, then covered the spaghetti and worked it together. Setting both pans on the lowest setting, I cleaned up the dishes and headed for my cabin to shower, shave and dress. I had a note in my pocket to borrow Jib's pickup and head out to get the folding chairs at the rental office. When I called Mae, she agreed to take the roasters when she and Bonnie left, leaving me free to set up chairs and help Nate.

It was already 1:00 when I finally arrived at the church and backed up to the front doors, where the four Spellman boys were waiting to help unload. I noticed Mae and several women coming and going downstairs, shuttling food and supplies. About 1:15 Nate asked if we'd park our cars in the grassy field adjacent to the church, leaving more room for the funeral guests.

I had just moved the truck when the hearse took my place with the directors enlisting aid to bring the casket into the sanctuary. Avis and her family followed in a second car just minutes behind, seeming to open the flood gates for others right behind them. Both the parking lot and the church filled very quickly, attesting to Nate's wisdom for providing extra parking and seating. I was standing alone outside watching the procession when Mae and Bonnie each took one of my arms and guided me inside to a seat.

She had a clean smell about her, no perfume but a clean soapy smell. Like someone right out of the shower, I could not help but drink it in as she walked at my side. In just over 48 hours Bonnie had stolen a heart that had never been given away except to Jesus.

Faith was playing the piano, providing background to the sounds of murmured greetings and acknowledgments, the scraping of chairs, and coughs and cleared throats in the sanctuary. Here and there a sob could be heard of one overcome with distress.

At exactly 2:00 Nate took the podium looking pastoral, but not grave or sorrowful, in his gray suit. He nodded to Faith who struck a chord for a hymn at the family's request and we all stood and sang along. At the front, between the raised dais and the front rows of chairs, the casket had been placed with flowers on both sides, an American flag covering it. The handout which gave some of Ted's life story indicated he had served in Desert Storm. Occasionally, tearful murmurs came from his children and others present.

Nate began with the usual acknowledgments and thanks to the guests present, then read the obituary slowly giving each time to create a picture of the man's life in their imagination. Then he opened his Bible and read from Jeremiah 29:11, "For I know the plans I have for you," says the Lord. "They are plans for good and not for disaster, to give you a future and a hope."

He hesitated before continuing, then said, "Jesus has plans for each of us, plans that often make no sense to us while we are living them. Plans that were made before we were born, sometimes for a purpose yet to come. His promise to us is that they are for good, they are to give us hope for the future. If I may, I'd like to share with you an example."

"A little over two years ago my wife died. I was shattered and broken, I felt I had no reason to live, and no purpose. When I arrived here just a short time ago, I was running away, not to something, but from something. At least that was how it felt to me. However, God already had a plan, a place, a purpose, and now a person in mind when I stopped at the Widespot.

The room grew quiet, enwrapped in his story.

Pastor Nate continued. "He placed me here among you for this very purpose, at just the time He knew of your need, and now has filled the hole in my heart with a new love. Mae has agreed to marry me." He then paused. As unlikely as a wedding announcement seemed at a funeral, it fit into the fabric of hope he was weaving.

"What I hope you hear today, and take home with you, is the promise that this fleeting life is not all there is for we who believe. We will soon be reunited, but in the meanwhile, there are plans already in place to comfort us and heal our wounds."

He stopped speaking for a moment, then invited those who had known and loved Ted to relive with us their happier memories of him. In the beginning most were reluctant to share, but as time went on and laughter broke the spell of loss, more and more joined in. I felt as if I had known him and looked forward to knowing him better when we both walked with Jesus in eternity.

An hour later the last speaker seated himself and Faith began to play the final hymn. Afterward, Pastor Nate closed us in prayer and reminded us that the savory smells were coming from downstairs.

Two of those things which God provides to wounded hearts are friends and food. It takes energy to suffer pain, physical or emotional, and as unlikely as it seems, emotion breeds physical hunger. And friends, of course, encourage and help us bear life's burdens. The entire congregation spent most of the afternoon eating, laughing and crying together before heading home with much less of a feeling of loss.

PART NINE

As surely as winter follows autumn, Sunday morning came right on the heels of Saturday afternoon. To those who did the cooking and clean up, and to we who folded and returned the extra chairs to the rental agency, it came especially early. "The faithful," that's what those are called who can be counted on to make every effort to do what is right.

That's what I saw when I got to the church a little before 10:00, the faithful arriving after going home to chores late last evening or doing them when they awoke early this morning to get ready for service. The little extra effort they put into their lives to do that which we were called to do. I was proud of them for making a point to come on time after getting their kids ready, milking the cow, or throwing feed to their herds. I felt lazy by comparison.

Mae and Bonnie were already seated beside Buffy, Faith and the children when I came in. They motioned me over and made room between them. Faith's second backup was at her station softly playing the piano as the last few were seated. Our sanctuary was a single large rectangular room, having a small raised dais at the front. The pews were arranged in two sections on the hardwood floor, leaving a wide aisle in the middle between them and narrower ones on each side. The walking space between the aisles had been carpeted to minimize the sound of footsteps and prevent slippery floors in winter.

I estimated full capacity at about eight per pew on each side and about ten deep, making the seating about 150-160. The way people are, they naturally leave space between men, families, and visitors, reducing our seating to a comfortable one hundred or so. Each week since Pastor Nate had lead us, we were nearly full.

Pastor Nate opened us in prayer as usual, then joined us in a hymn before introducing the church board, Buck, Glen, and Al, who had some church business to discuss. First was to establish a church budget which included building maintenance, the pastor's salary, the establishment of a benevolent fund, and the need for more seating.

Buck took the lead, laying out the general need for ongoing maintenance, utilities, and improvements. He filled the congregation in on the youth project that had sealed and stripped the parking lot. A round of applause for the youth was given. Then their plan to utilize the grain field next door as a football field and picnic area. The land had been donated to the church years before by the Hawkins family. Beth (Sadie) Hawkins raised her head only slightly in acknowledgment as others stared surprised.

Labor and equipment to prepare and plant the ground had been donated, however, the cost to provide seed, install sprinklers, and erect goal posts had to be budgeted. He promised to have the figures to discuss and bring to vote within two weeks.

Glen stood next, addressing the condition of sanctuary and proposed upgrades and improvements, including more seating. He promised prices for consideration and discussion at a regular business meeting.

Finally, Al stood, addressing the congregation with a need to prayerfully consider a reasonable, sustainable salary for their pastor. A printed bulletin would be available for each family to take home and discuss privately at the close of service today.

Buck then called Nate forward and handed him a sealed envelope to present to Avis and her family from the church and the community in their time of need. It contained the contents of Mae's fishbowl plus many other large donations from around the valley, totaling several thousand dollars. Only the board knew the exact amount.

"Used of God" was the title given to Pastor Nate's sermon. Nate laid the groundwork that each of God's creations have a place, a part to play, a purpose for existing. He started with examples of the smallest creatures and their function in nature's continuing cycle.

He asked, by a raising of hands, how many liked and enjoyed house flies, bringing chuckles and outhouse humor into the room. Next he asked the same question of spiders, gnats, grasshoppers, etc. After a minute he asked how many enjoyed birds, then cats and dogs, as he continued to expand the natural food chain.

Nothing, nothing in creation is there by chance or unnecessary. I heard the word 'appendix' murmured, to which Nate had a ready answer. "Just because you don't know the purpose doesn't mean it does not have one." A corporate laugh ensued.

Everyone knew bees were necessary for pollination but none enjoyed their sting or saw the necessity for wasps. As it became clear that function had its purpose, Nate moved to the Bible. "Open Isaiah to chapter 45 if you will and read along with me," he asked. "The verse begins with God speaking, with Him laying the groundwork for using Cyrus, King of Persia, as His instrument."

Most, being country folks with fences, corner posts, survey monuments, and established property lines could relate. Nate stood silent for a few seconds, facing the congregation, making eye contact with many.

"So then, my friends," he finally continued, "how are you being 'used of God'? Do you have a desire to be used more? Or do you even know where you belong in His plan? Are you being used now? Would you think about it this week, maybe make some notes, and we will return to discuss it more next week."

Pastor Nate finished up in prayer, asking any with specific or urgent needs to remain after service and meet with him. I could tell by the buzz and the clusters of people in small groups that the service had touched hearts and opened eyes.

Nate was still at the front, having been button-holed by Beth Hawkins, before he could leave for his usual place at the door. Buck and the board were standing in his place shaking hands and passing out bulletins as people began to leave.

As I left, I shook Glen's hand and speaking quietly I said, "let me know when you get the numbers together for the additional seating. Maybe I can help with that."

Bonnie was right ahead of me with Mae as the crowd began to spread out, walking toward their cars. I caught her elbow, causing both she and Mae to stop and turn toward me.

"What are you doing for dinner?" I asked, already turning red as others picked up on my question. I tried to clarify, "I mean, with the Widespot closed, we have nowhere to go to eat."

Bonnie let me stew in my own juice for a few seconds before smiling and answering my question with one of her own. "Are you asking me out to dinner, or are you looking for a recommendation of somewhere to go?" She could be so cruel. I was back in junior high again whenever I was around her.

"I was hoping that if you had no other plans, that maybe the four of us might drive into town and eat someone else's special for a change."

I did not wait for her answer, "Mae do you and Nate have plans?"

"I'm afraid so, Bum," she said, "Nate has already accepted an invitation to the Bakers for dinner tonight."

That left me standing there without a clue until Bonnie took my arm and smiled into my eyes and said, "that just leaves you and me, I guess."

Mae smiled, then said over her shoulder, "take the truck and have fun!"

Jib's old Ford was as dependable as a dog and looked like one too. It appeared that the road dirt held it together, and the extra gear rattling around in the back made it sound like a heap. I was embarrassed to be driving a 'date' anywhere in it, she, however, seemed right at home.

We had gone back to our cabins and changed into more casual clothes, and giving our toothbrushes a workout. She was waiting beside the truck looking twenty when I came out, feeling fifteen and looking sixty. I did remember to open her door for her before climbing into the dusty cab.

"Sorry about the truck," I said, "we normally just use it around the café, never gets cleaned up.

"Reminds me of home," she said softly, leaning back into the seat, her arm out the open window and her eyes closed. The old truck didn't have air conditioning and the September afternoon was sultry and hot, making air movement our only option. I watched as the air caressed her short blond hair, unable to ruin its natural beauty. I felt very self-conscious just being alone with her, I could almost hear my own heart beating in my chest.

"Where's home?" I asked trying to sound casual, but failing badly.

"Born in Illinois," she answered, "grew up in Kansas. Kansas is where I call home."

"Family? I continued, trying to get a feel for who and what she had been before last week.

"Mom and Dad are gone, got a half-brother somewhere in the military... we're not close. How about you?" she asked turning the tables.

"Only child," I volunteered. "Born with a silver spoon," I said trying to keep it light, "born in California, but this is my home."

"You are happy here," she said, making a statement, "I envy you."

"I am," I agreed, "found happiness when I wasn't looking for it."

"Jesus?" She asked.

"Yes, Jesus," I answered, testifying of my faith, "you?"

Bonnie hesitated a little, "I'm not so sure. I was once, but now I have doubts."

I saw tears in the corner of her blue eyes, the 'why' questions I suppose, like Pastor Nate told us. I expect he'd call it a crisis of faith or something. I took care to listen and not volunteer opinions, a trait that I was trying hard to develop. I nodded, "we all have those sometimes," I agreed.

We rode together for an hour without speaking, unwilling to open ourselves up to scrutiny or ridicule.

"You ever get lonesome?" she asked out of the blue.

I wanted to say 'not until I met you', but didn't. "I used to, that's why I just bummed around, trying to find out where I fit," I said honestly. "I thought it was people I was looking for to give meaning to my life, but I found it was Jesus who was missing in my life."

"And... you've found that here? Here at the Widespot?" she asked sounding kind of desperate. I pulled over at a turnout and shut off the motor.

"No, yes. I mean I have found Jesus, and salvation, and friendships, and meaning in service to Him. But, I feel He has something more waiting for me. Did you listen to the sermon today?" She nodded.

"I feel that maybe I haven't fulfilled all that I was created for yet."

"Like Cyrus?" she asked.

"Yup, just like him. Maybe some special reason why I was created more than what I know now." She smiled, "I like that."

We drove all the way into Coeur d'Alene, then parked down by the lake in a lot downtown. It was after 5:00 and I was hungry. "Been here before?" I asked.

"Didn't stop, just got a burger and rode through," she answered. When you are alone and on the road, things tend to get complicated if you stay in towns."

"You mean cops, men, what?" I asked trying to understand. This was the second time since we met that she alluded to being careful on the road.

"I mean men mostly, trying to pick you up, offer you something but meaning something else. A woman alone seems fair game to some, vulnerable. I nodded, wondering how she'd become so cynical and mistrusting, if she'd been victimized.

"Hungry?" I asked.

"Starving," she answered, "you?"

"Yes," I answered smiling. "How does prime rib sound to you? She smiled, her eyes twinkling, "you just get paid or something?"

"Nope, not in a while, but I've saved some for a special occasion."

"And...?" she asked.

"And..." I answered, "this is it."

We walked the downtown which sported a dozen eating places, a few bars, but mostly tourist shops and galleries before stopping at a bistro I had tried before. There was a bar, a restaurant, and patio dining available. We elected to sit inside where it was more private, where we could visit.

Inside it was old school; dark wood, dim lighting, spacious seating, and somewhat rustic atmosphere with pictures of locomotives, miners, loggers, and such lining the walls from days gone by. The waitress brought us an oversized menu and a glass of white wine each. Northern Idaho has a rich heritage of rugged individualists who challenged the land searching for their fortunes in mines, logging camps, railroad construction, and raising the crops to feed themselves and others.

When she asked about me, I sensed a real desire to know about my past, so I shared things that I seldom shared. Not just events, but also my feelings, my victories and disappointments, my heart. Bonnie was a good listener, knowing when to ask for clarification or agree, but also knowing when to remain silent and just listen.

When she asked me about my plans for the future, I replied honestly that I hadn't really considered it. For the past several years I had been content to take it as it came, day by day, enjoying the challenges and joys each brought with it. She said she envied me that, the peace I had found.

I could tell that she was still searching, hoping that she may copy someone else's pattern for happiness. The waitress returned and took our orders, then disappeared.

I could almost feel her withdraw and raise her guard when I asked about her. She was thirty six, although she could have passed for twenty six, had graduated from junior college in Kansas while living at home with her parents. She had moved to Portland and completed her education in marine biology, remaining there working with state and federal fisheries for a half dozen years before moving on.

It became obvious that she didn't want to discuss her reason for leaving, so I let it drop. I was disappointed, I had bared my soul hoping for the same openness and honesty from her, but received the equivalent of a job application in return.

Our waitress brought our food and refilled our drinks. Instinctively I took her hand and bowed my head to bless the food, but found her reluctant to share the moment. Her hand, covered by my own, remained tense and ready to withdraw as if this small intimacy violated her personal space. The food was delicious but the mood, for me at least, was lost.

We talked superficially through dessert, then returned to the park where we enjoyed watching the broad expanse of the lake together. The walk on the beach, holding hands and laughing, sharing our hearts, maybe even a first kiss... the thoughts I had enjoyed while on the drive down, were gone. I felt resentful on our trip home, but tried not to show it, keeping up the senseless chatter that society calls conversation. At Mae's house, she smiled, squeezed my hand, then slipped quickly out the far door thanking me 'for a wonderful day'.

In my cabin I felt hurt, almost betrayed, having accepted her thanks the same way one would have from an aging aunt who spent the day away from her nursing home. I knew I was being foolish, that my feelings were magnified by my own failed expectations.

I found myself turning to Jesus, asking questions, sharing my hurt, praying for understanding and then... I had a revelation. It wasn't all about me, I was the one who had felt at peace, complete, whole... it was about this young woman who felt alone and incomplete, who was needy and did not have Jesus' peace in her heart. God had not brought her as a gift for me, but possibly that I could be a gift to her. Maybe to provide what she seemed to be lacking.

I had already begun the Monday morning routine when Mae joined me through the rear door, paper under her arm.

"Morning Mae," I said in my usual manner.

"Morning Bum," she replied, a furrow creasing her brow as she sat at the counter with a cup in her hand.

"Bonnie's gone," she said matter-of-factly, "left before I got up, left us a note." She handed me the handwritten copy.

"Thank you for everything, tell everyone for me that I will miss them and that you'll always be part of my life. Love, Bonnie."

Just like that, she, her bike and meager belongings were on the road again, searching for something we hadn't had to give. I returned to the kitchen where I prayed for her safety, direction, and fulfillment, and for myself... relief from the pain I felt in my heart.

PART TEN

Buffy walked in whistling and smiling. I wanted to club him. Didn't he know I was suffering? Couldn't he tell I had a hole in my heart? Well, probably not.

"Mornin' Bum," he said with a grin, "what's cookin'?" Then he laughed at his own joke.

Mae broke the levity, "how is Faith feeling these days?"

"Much better, no morning sickness after the Doc got her some medicine," he answered.

"Bonnie is gone," Mae continued, "please let Faith know we can use her help anytime she is up to it."

"Want me to call her?" Buff asked.

"No, we'll make it fine today," Mae answered, "but tomorrow if she is feeling like it."

Don Taylor was first through the door, sporting a grin and a hand full of mail. "Here for the free breakfast," he bragged.

"Sorry Don," Mae answered, "that was just for last week. Poor old Bum ran out of money."

He pretended to pout but ordered bacon, eggs scrambled, and English muffin with honey, grilled. Bill was the next to enter, looking at Don with distaste, "I see Don beat me," he said.

Don laughed, "yes I did but the free breakfast deal was just for last week, so we are both up early for nothin'."

I pretended to take offense, "what do you mean for nuthin'? You are right on time for a nice breakfast," I said smiling.

The same ritual happened again a few minutes later when Tom DeGrange joined the others at the counter. I stepped out of the kitchen, feeling a need to clarify. I told them of the little joke I had played on Bonnie and how it had backfired on me and that she had moved on. All replied that they'd miss her.

Our breakfast hour was typical with the exception of a car load of students with big appetites and Glen Gardner, who was not a frequent guest, for breakfast. As time permitted, I left the grill to Buff and stepped aside to where Glen waited for me.

"I got those figures," he said. "We can fit in four more rows of pews, one on each side," showing me his drawing. "Eight total. We can pick up some used ones in Spokane for $250 each or have them built locally to match the old ones for around $400." I nodded.

"What else is on your Christmas list, Glen?" I asked.

"Well, we've discussed new carpet runners, but the pews are a bigger priority."

I handed him a check for $5,000 from my trust account and said, "use it however you think is best, but keep it confidential please."

We'd returned with no spaghetti from the previous day, any that had been left over was taken home by those in need, so we began the week with a clean slate and a need for a lunch and dinner menu.

Luckily I was busy most of the morning and my mood improved as I tried not to dwell on myself by serving the needs of others. I went to the walk-in cooler finding only a front shoulder and a few cuts off a rear quarter remaining. That left me only a few practical options.

I saved a few cuts of steak, then began boning the ribs for stew while Buffy readied the vegetables. The water heated to boiling, I added the bones with salt, then began the process of dredging the meat in seasoned flour, then browning it on the grill.

The phone rang and I could hear Mae speaking in the other room. She came into the kitchen smiling. "That was Buck, they'll be over this afternoon with a steer, he wanted you to know."

A thought came to mind, 'He doth provide'. I imagine that when we question His provision, He sometimes gives us a little reminder that He is there and still at work. A word came to mind... 'faithbuilder'.

I made three nice rolled roasts from the rear quarter and boned the remainder, adding the bones to the boiling water, then married the lean meat with that from the front quarter. About 10:00 the bones were removed, leaving only a tasty beef stock ready to accept the meat and vegetables. I dipped out about a quart of stock and started a roux while the meat continued to boil.

I thickened the stock with flour and corn starch, browning it while stirring, then added it back to the main pot. In effect, it turned the stock into a brown gravy with meat. When we added the vegetables we had to re-season the mixture as they act like little sponges, hungry for salt. By 11:00, two pots were simmering and giving off an aroma that could have been bottled and sold. The roasts were in the oven slow cooking for a French dip special later in the day.

Faith arrived before the first noon-time guest, looking well and full of energy. Buffy spent a few minutes with her before rejoining me in the kitchen. Apparently all three children were in school now, making day care unnecessary until the baby was born. I enjoyed seeing the youthful happiness which Faith had brought to Buffy's countenance and the joy he had brought to replace the pain of loss to hers.

Pastor Nate was our first lunch guest, seating himself at the counter and commenting on the smells of the stew coming from the kitchen. I grilled him a cheese sandwich and Mae served it with a bowl of stew and a nice dill pickle on the side. I overheard him share that the church had ordered eight new pews and was looking into replacing the carpeting as well. I smiled to myself, taking care not to let my pride take hold of me.

Doug, our tow truck driver was next in, with a wreck on the roll back on its way to the junk yard. He joined Nate at the counter, introducing himself before ordering a grilled ham and cheese and stew. Nate invited him to come by the church and look around when he was passing, in a way that left it as a pleasant option for some slow afternoon in the near future. Buck and crew entered next, filling up two tables, after washing up. The two older sons joined them after hanging two nice halves of beef in our cooler.

"Smells like beef in here," he said, a little too loudly. In his own way I think he needed to hear that the beef industry was alive and well. Mae greeted them, poured water and handed out menus to the six. I took a short break to join them and thank Buck for the steer.

"Been hanging ten days, should be fork tender if you cook it right," he declared.

"I'll try and do it justice," I answered.

Mae served their stew 'family style' sitting a big mixing bowl holding a couple of gallons in the middle of the table. I grilled up a loaf of bread, with ham and cheese, making a couple of sandwiches each that were served on a couple of platters. Water and milk finished up their spread.

Buffy had taken the roasts out at about rare, allowing them to continue cooking in the pan on the side board. Buck must have caught it out of the corner of his eye because he questioned why they were eating pig when there was roast beef to be had.

As the pace picked up, both Mae and Faith scampered to keep up. Buff and I had the easy part for a change for those who were wanting the special. He finally began to buss tables and refill drinks to help out, while I remained at the grill.

About 2:00 my world fell apart. Tom and Bill came in together just as we had served our last table, taking a seat at the counter. Their faces showed their pain and concern before they spoke. We four and Nate still remained. We heard the story with unbelief, the car that Doug had been hauling had sideswiped Bonnie's bicycle, then lost control and rolled killing both the driver and his passenger.

Autopsies would confirm their initial suspicion, that they were driving impaired. Bonnie had been life flighted to Spokane in critical condition. Neither officer had been able to identify her at the scene because of blood and bruising. It was only now, as the investigation progressed, that they had found her identification and returned to notify us. No one hesitated as Nate lead us in prayer, then we each took our turn as tears ran down our cheeks. Our hearts claimed Jesus' mercy and love, asking for His healing hand for Bonnie.

PART ELEVEN

The 'why' question surged to the forefront of my consciousness, attempting to discredit God, to destroy my faith, to undermine my spiritual strength as we drove south toward Spokane. Nate had graciously agreed to drive and Buffy claimed to have things well in hand at the Widespot. His words of consolation bounced off me like golf balls off concrete.

Nate's Bible quotations meant for comfort sounded trite and were ineffective in providing peace. In the scheme of things, we had only known each other a week, but it was enough to awaken dreams of a future together. I had never known pain so acute, so personal and cruel. The scars left from my parents death had long since lost their sting.

"Oh, Lord, my God, when I in silent wonder..." Nate began to hum, saying nothing. Soon I picked up on the tune and found myself humming also as tears followed one another down my cheeks.

Did I know her last name? I was jolted as I realized that this woman who had stolen my heart had never told me her name. How could that be? How can one care so much about someone they knew so little about, I thought to myself.

Then I thought of Jesus, how He loved us before we first loved Him. How His great love for us was so one sided, loving us before we were born, before we claimed Him, even those who never chose to love Him.

I called the café, Mae answered. "Do you know Bonnie's name?" I asked.

"Smith, I think, only spelled with a Y, Smythe," she said. "Let me ask Tom."

As she came back on the line she confirmed Bonnie Lee Smythe, she repeated slowly, no record of next of kin.

"She has a brother somewhere but they are not close," I said. "No idea his name or where he may be." Somehow I felt relieved at knowing this little bit about her life, this small thing seemed to give me hope.

It was 3:45 when we passed through Post Falls heading west toward Spokane on the interstate. Nate was pushing the speed limit by five and sometimes ten miles an hour, I knew that and appreciated it. I knew were he alone, he'd have stayed under the posted speed.

Spokane is a sizable town, maybe a half million or so, I am not sure. But it was large enough to require another call home to find out which hospital she had been taken to.

Isn't it odd that we seem to think that if we are with someone things will turn out alright? How somehow if we had been with them we could have prevented or minimized the tragedy? We always rush to the bedside of a dying relative as though our presence would make a difference in God's plan.

When we arrived, Nate asked at the desk for Bonnie Smythe and was given her room number in ICU. We arrived on the floor, facing a nurses station, as we got off the elevator. It occupied a spot in the center of a spacious room, with smaller rooms surrounding it in all directions, like the spokes of a wheel.

Nate spoke slowly and in muted tones, identifying himself as her clergy. When the nurses eyes fixed on me, I lied, "I'm her brother," just as if I had said it all of my life. The words felt strange coming out of my mouth, while knowing them to be lies.

She accepted us at face value, "she's in an induced coma, I'm afraid," she said, then adding, "to help prevent swelling to her brain."

May we spend a few minutes with her?" Nate asked.

"Of course," the nurse answered, "but she will not know you are here.

Now, I've been around some, been in hospitals before and have a working knowledge of the human body and the practical side of some of our life support equipment. Never would I have been prepared for the scene which faced us as we entered the room. Tubes, monitors, wires, lights, and a myriad of noises coming from each. Emotion made sight difficult and speech impossible as I gazed at her lying motionless in a cocoon of bandages, eyes closed, breathing with the aid of a respirator.

The nurse was speaking softly to Nate, "it was necessary to remove her spleen to stop the internal bleeding, her kidneys have shut down, and there is bleeding inside her skull. The trauma often causes the kidneys to stop so that is not a concern, and the internal injuries seem under control following surgery. The extent of the damage to the brain and the bleeding remain unknown." She squeezed my hand, then returned to her station, leaving us alone.

We sat on either side of the bed, taking her hands in ours as we began to pray. I asked God to forgive my deceit and to not charge her with my sin. I could hear Nate praying also but could not discern the words. After a few minutes, which seemed like hours, I felt exhausted, spent, drained of emotion and feeling. I just held her hand and watched as her eyes moved under her lids. There was no indication that she was alive except her regulated breathing and the REM movement of her blue eyes.

As I sat I thought about prayer; it's types, it's value, it's personal meaning to me. When I have prayed for myself, I have sometimes felt selfish, unworthy, and have minimized my requests. Not because of my belief in God's inability to answer any need, but of my own sense of greed.

Not so when I pray as an intercessor for others. I feel liberated to ask for whatever is needed, as I had today for Bonnie. The value of our prayers is obvious when they are answered according to our requests, less so when it appears unheard or answered in God's own time and way.

As I sat, holding her hand and half listening to Nate pray, my mind was scattered as butterflies fleeing from a meadow in alarm, coming to rest here and there before taking wing again. Dynamic. That word came to mind. I attempted to wrap my head around it's meaning in current context.

'The dynamics of prayer', what did that mean to me? I apologize that I seem to be running afield here, but my mind, my heart was unsettled and illogical. I remembered a principle from a long ago lecture in physics, 'for every action, there is an equal and opposite reaction'. In God's economy, everything 'is' that ever was, nothing is ever lost or consumed, the total sum of all things remains in balance throughout the universe.

So then, I thought, when I invest in prayer something does happen, must happen according to God's plan. I may have mentioned earlier that I was gifted with a scientific mind. What then happens, or is happening as Nate and I pray? While in retrospect, this seems like a long way around the lake, I am attempting to have you walk the pathway with me.

I do not pretend to know how the mind of God works. How He can hear us today and have already prepared an answer to the question we are just now asking. Someday, maybe. It seemed impossible to me that this event, which was crushing my heart, had been preplanned and its outcome already determined before my pleas and prayers were heard.

And yet, we are commanded to pray. To what purpose, I asked myself, knowing that I was also asking God. The answer was immediate and as loud in my head as thunder, "for My purpose, to learn dependence, to grow in faith, to give Me glory."

Wow! I felt like Job getting his due reprimand. Chastised was the word that filled my head. I want to make it clear that I consider myself a man of faith, a true believer, a Christian pilgrim doing my best to walk uprightly. I do admit that when confronted, my faith withers like the leaves on Jesus' fig tree.

I returned to prayer, this time more audibly, with renewed conviction, with a sense of hope and not futility in my heart.

The nurse had returned and stood watching and listening as we poured out our hearts. As I lifted my head, I saw tears rimming her eyes, her own lips moving, before she laid her hand gently on my shoulder.

"I'm sorry," she said, "you'll have to go, we are taking her down for an MRI to try and determine the extent of damage to her brain, it may take an hour or more. Nate must have heard also, for he stood and joined me as I walked toward the door.

I stopped and turned toward her, "I am not her brother," I admitted, "but I love her anyway." She nodded.

"I know," she said, "he has been contacted in Maryland, but is unable to come. He was listed as 'next of kin' on a slip in her wallet. You must be Bum Roberts, listed to call in case of emergency. I nodded, tears reforming in my eyes.

Emotionally drained, Nate and I turned to food for healing, eating copious amounts from the steam table in their cafeteria before regaining enough stamina to converse.

Why is it that those chosen of God always seem to boast a fatherly demeanor? Nate was probably only fifteen years my senior, but imparted a sense of stability and wisdom worthy of an octogenarian. On the drive, when he had said, "she is in God's hands," it seemed hollow and almost condescending. Now I nodded in the agreement that I had known all along. I felt drawn to relate to Nate what I had felt and 'nearly' heard in her room earlier, when questioning the value of prayer. He gave me an auspicious smile and simply said, "been there, done that."

Having more presence of mind than myself, Nate called Mae and reported what we knew and where it seemed to be going. He asked her to continue to pray before telling her not to expect us back tonight.

Seasons. Now this word flashed across the screen in my head.

Seasons, I thought, what are seasons? They are both the beginning and end, each with a purpose and each temporary. I did not like any thought of temporary. It hurt to think that my season of knowing

Bonnie might be so brief.

We use the term 'scatter brained' in conversation, usually in a negative way, to denote inconsistency and undependability. My mind was drawn to Bonnie's first breakfast order... "and scatter the potatoes" she had said, a term for letting hash-browns brown individually and acquire an extra crispness. God was letting my mind heal and season as it fluttered and flew like those butterflies.

My musings were interrupted by Nate, "we better get a room for the night before we return upstairs," he suggested. The Travel Lodge was over-priced for it's amenities, but had the draw of being within waking distance to the hospital. We shared a single room with two queens, took advantage of the complementary tooth brushes, paste, soap and razors that were offered, before returning to ICU.

It had been an hour and a half since we had left. Bonnie rested back in her room looking just as she had earlier. Her nurse had gone off shift, another taking her place, stood in conversation with a doctor in her room as we entered.

Doctor Mason, from the name on his coat, turned toward us and identified himself. Apparently the previous nurse had cut any red tape which may have prevented us from acquiring medical information, because he began to speak candidly.

"The bleeding has stopped," said the doctor.

"Praise God!" Nate said aloud, causing Dr. Mason to smile and say "indeed." He continued down a mental checklist of important findings; heart beat steady, blood pressure normal, breathing still being assisted for her comfort, incision seems to be healing nicely, no sign of additional bleeding internally, severe bruising to her ribs and back, and more which I can't remember.

All seemed hopeful until he changed his tone of voice and began a second list. "There's a hematoma in her skull the size of a walnut putting pressure on her brain, severe bruising to her left cortex, and a clot behind her left optic nerve, possibly from the bruising. We'll have to wait, and pray, that there is no permanent damage which will impair her respiratory function, that the clot will dissipate on its own without damaging the optic nerve, and that her body will absorb the one on her brain before it causes a stroke or permanent damage."

So, I thought, she is not out of the woods yet. Many of the more important things are still up in the air.

His voice became soft and caring as his report concluded, "we can't use blood thinners because of the earlier surgery and possibility of a new round of bleeding. A stroke is a real possibility for which we have no medical answer.

Nate spoke softly, "as always, she remains in God's hands." Mason nodded and patted us on our sagging shoulders before walking away.

Nate and I returned to our respective positions bedside and resumed prayer. Again, it seemed I had been drained of energy and vitality in the enterprise. I remembered my hypothesis from earlier, that nothing in our universe is gained or lost, just transformed. I hoped that my energy had been transformed into an effective prayer for Bonnie's safe recovery.

We left our phone number at the nurse's station before leaving and returning to our room, where Nate called Mae once again. He went through the entire laundry list from memory, the good, the bad, and the ugly... before hanging up. I remember being exhausted but feeling a need to talk so I broached a more upbeat subject.

"Have you and Mae chosen a date yet?"

Nate smiled, reveling in the very thought of being united with Mae, then said, "October 7th if God wills."

If God wills... something we should all consider when making any statement, I thought to myself. Wasn't Bonnie a very real example? As God wills, always.

One can speculate about God's will in 'what if's' all day, not accomplishing a thing. What if she had stayed longer, what if the car had left earlier or later, what if it had missed her or killed her at the scene. What

I was beginning to see was a pattern, a pattern too great for a human mind to conceive or understand. The old 'everything happens for a reason' thing, which is no answer at all to the question 'why'. I had come full circle as my eyes grew heavy and consciousness fled before me.

I awoke to the sound of Nate's phone ringing, disoriented. It was the morning of the third day. I have no recollection of the second at all, blank. As Nate tried to filled me in, it remained as though looking into a steamy mirror, hardly recognizing anything. Apparently the second had been uneventful, little had seemed to change in our routine or in her condition.

My mind had refused to accept and register events and therefore had not recorded them in memory – how very odd, I thought. Today I felt rested and alive as I showered and shaved, while Nate called home asking for Mae to get the prayer chain alerted to Bonnie's need. We accepted the offering of the continental breakfast of waffles, fruit, cereal, juice and coffee at the motel, grateful to have something quick and easy.

The original nurse was on the floor when we got off the elevator, giving me a sense of security and comfort. We had been with her just a short time before she was taken away for a follow-up MRI. We were snapped from our surreal world into reality when a page came for us to report to the business office.

A heavy-set, middle aged woman greeted us pleasantly at first. She apparently had the unenviable job of pursuing collections from deadbeats, indigents, the uninsured, transients, and unemployed. Bonnie fell well within the bounds of several of these descriptions. She was hopeful that 'Mr. in-case-of-emergency' may placate her superior's desire to be fiscally responsible to its board of directors. Nate came along for moral support, having no doubt encountered such a person himself while his wife was hospitalized.

"We see here that she had named you to be contacted in case of emergency, is that correct?"

"I guess it is, must be if you say so, I have no personal knowledge," I replied noncommittally.

"Then you are not a blood relative or employer?"

"I am not, just a recent friend," I answered honestly.

"So," she seemed offended by my answers, "you have no financial interest in the patient? Is that correct?"

I was beginning to remember that I once had a temper. "Financial, no, personal, yes – and the 'patient' has a name," I said firmly.

Oh, I'm sorry, I didn't mean to offend you," she said back tracking.

"No offense taken," I said, trying hard to sound genuine.

"Do you know her brother," she asked?

"I do not, she mentioned him once, saying that they were estranged," I replied.

Nate finally spoke, "pardon my intrusion please, but if there is nothing else we can help you with, we need to get back to her room."

"Yes, of course," she said, resignation in her voice at having lost another attempt to recover medical costs, "I do appreciate your time."

I felt sorry for her so I dangled a carrot, "you might contact the Sheriff's office and get the name of the responsible parties and their insurance carrier's name," I suggested. "They were both killed, I understand, but if they were insured you may have right of recovery."

She brightened noticeably, "thank you," she said, "I certainly will."

On the elevator on the way up, Nate smiled and said, "good thinking back there, I hope they were well covered."

I nodded, mentally tallying a 'best guess' estimate for medical treatment to date. Bonnie had not returned when we arrived so I spent a few minutes visiting with her nurse. I found that she was a Christian who had been praying for all of her patients by name for years.

"And..." I said, "what have been the results?"

She hesitated, attempting to formulate a correct answer before speaking. "They are always answered," she said, almost defiantly. Then she softened her tone, "God always heals those He loves, some here on earth, others in heaven."

Well said," Nate interrupted, "may I have permission to use that in a sermon?"

Nurse Katie smiled, then said, "certainly."

When Bonnie was returned to her room, it took several minutes to reconnect, adjust, and verify all of her equipment before we were allowed to enter. A few minutes later, Doctor Mason followed carrying the usual clipboard and a smile on his face.

Both Nate and I took notice at his demeanor as he began to go through the now familiar list once again. Several items had moved from the left side to the right, into the 'good' column.

"Swelling is down, no indication of further bleeding, and the pressure behind her eye is diminishing. Jury is still out on respiration, but we are hopeful. There is no way to know the extent of brain damage until she is brought out of the coma. We may try and remove the trach later today which will give some indication of brain function in that area."

Nurse Katie smiled and winked. I nearly laughed.

"You two keep up the good work," Dr. Mason said to us with a smile before exiting the room.

"Good man," I commented to the room.

"God's instrument," the nurse corrected.

PART TWELVE

I had seldom thought of mankind in those terms. In "Christianspeak", among the believers, such terms as 'used by God' or 'in God's service' were used to refer to a great diversity of things. From the woman in the nursery to the underpaid janitor or lay preacher, the missionaries in foreign lands, to those like Nate who committed themselves to Him, many served in their own way.

How interesting that God might similarly gift a man as a doctor or research scientist, knowing that to non-believers He had created His own competition. Who would get credit for healing, God? Unlikely. More likely the medical staff who were often more than willing to take the bow.

While we were at lunch, they removed the breathing tube. Bonnie struggled at first, her body having become lazy and dependent upon the machine, but finally it resumed its role to regulate her respiration. It was a blessing of untold proportions to both us and the staff, indicating a smaller chance of severe brain damage. Her left eye, however was not as reactive to light stimulus as the other and showed itself still red with blood.

Nate and I took our positions and resumed prayer, beginning this time with praise and thankfulness, which I, at the least, had previously overlooked. Nate called Mae once more, filling in the blanks, giving hope and praise, then asking for continued prayer from the church.

As we returned from the cafeteria to the room, we caught Doctor

Mason making his rounds and asked for an update. Bonnie seemed somewhat agitated as opposed to her former condition, hands and legs moving occasionally in jerky motions, her breathing a little more labored. Dr. Mason informed us that they were cutting back on the drugs which had kept her comatose while allowing her to heal.

They would gradually try to awaken her, but in doing so she would begin to feel more of the pain that had been masked by drugs. He explained that the process would make her condition seem to worsen, possibly causing her to cry out as her body became aware of her injuries. For only a moment we joined hands, bowed our heads, and lifted up our hearts to God before he left the room.

Day four began like the others, shower, shave, grab a bite to eat, then return to the hospital with high hopes for good news. I had lost complete track of the days of the week and the month, I clung to the reality of knowing the year. It seemed months ago that we had left the Widespot.

That day we got our first autumn rain, a real thundershower, wetting both Nate and I to the skin on our short walk, but settling the dust out of the air. With my clothes dampened, all that remained was to dampen my spirits and that happened just as we got off the elevator.

I could hear Bonnie, crying out, sometimes cursing, or sobbing, her hands and feet restrained. Although still not alert, she was well aware of her injuries and struggled to physically fight against her restraints. Nurse Katie came right toward us, concern written on her face. "She's doing fine, try not to worry, it's just her nervous system being over-whelmed with her injuries."

My tears joined hers as my eyes filled, wishing I could somehow bear her burden. A thought came to mind... how many at the cross felt the same for Jesus? But it was He who must suffer for them instead.

Needless to say, our time with her ate wormholes in our hearts. Once she spoke, "please God help me." My heart broke, but also was encouraged that she knew and trusted in God. In the early afternoon she seemed to slip back into a coma, but more probably into an exhausted sleep. The nurses kept their distance, monitoring her on their machines rather than entering the room. My thought was that they too felt the emotion and attempted to distance themselves from it.

Late in the afternoon, Doctor Mason returned, checking each entry on her chart and each monitor carefully before turning to Nate and I.

"The worst may be over," he declared, lingering on the 'may'. "Her pain level has subsided, her body has become more accustomed to it, and her stats look promising," he said looking into her left eye.

I saw alarm register on his face as he looked again.

"Nurse!" he called, "page Doctor Druse stat!"

We waited, expecting explanation as the activity level on the floor increased. Dr. Mason was too busy to answer our questions, as they prepared to move Bonnie to another floor. When the elevator doors closed behind them, nurse Katie returned.

"The bleeder behind her eye has reopened and is restricting blood flow to her optic nerve. Doctor Druse is an ophthalmologist, an eye surgeon, one of our best. If he cannot restore the blood flow quickly she will be blind in her left eye."

I was in shock, crushed but not defeated as the saying goes, but feeling defeated all the same. God's plan, I thought feeling anger, why? There it was again, the "why" thing. I found myself pointing a shaking finger at God.

Mountains and valleys came to mind. Why mountains and valleys, I thought. To give you strength and endurance when climbing them, came the answer. Then a time of rest, reflection, and foresight while we sit at the summit. Followed by a time of descent where the walk is easy but the vision limited. At last back in the valley where you reside for a time in safety but without growth or vision before resuming your climb. Did God say that to me or did I think it, I wondered.

Katie, nurse Katie, checked on Bonnie for us before clocking out. She was still in surgery.

Nate urged me to rejoin him in prayer but I declined. I was pouting, angry, feeling helpless and lost. I rejected his attempts to comfort me, I wanted to feel the pain which fueled my anger against God.

The floor nurse finally brought news at 6:15, Bonnie was out of surgery and in recovery. She would be taken to a new room on the 3rd floor for observation. The nurse was unwilling or unable to offer us more information, directing us to the 3rd floor nurses' station.

On our short ride down I apologized to Nate, feeling guilty for my anger. We were not allowed into her room that evening but were encouraged that the surgery had gone as "well as could be expected." Whatever that meant. The statement just left the door open to worry without explanation. I slept little, then fitfully when I finally did.

When I awoke I realized, that rather than thanking God for saving her life and bringing her nearly back, I was angry at Him for not finishing the job on my schedule. Was it God's voice I heard or my own, "spoiled brat."

She was sitting up, her left eye and the side of her head covered in bandages, her right eye open. She kind of smiled as we entered the room. An 'I recognize you but I don't know what you are doing here' kind of smile. I said her name and she responded.

"How are you feeling?" Nate asked. She looked at him quizzically, "fine, I guess," she said, "my head hurts."

"Bum, why am I here? she asked. "What are you doing here? Where am I?"

I was encouraged to hear my name, but frightened at her memory loss. I took her hand, "you were hit on your bicycle by a drunken driver, you are in a hospital in Spokane. We are here to be with you," I finished while tearing up again.

"Am I alright?" she asked in a little girl voice, moving her hands and feet to make sure they worked.

"You'll be fine soon," I answered, "you are doing well."

"Is Mae here?" she asked.

"No," answered Nate, "she's back home praying for you."

"Oh," she said simply, then closed her eye and dozed off to sleep.

We ate lunch while she slept, called home with the good news, then returned to the hospital where we paged both doctors. Dr. Mason picked up the phone first.

"I haven't been by to see her yet today, Doctor Druse called me at home last night and gave her a good prognosis. He's the one you want to talk to first."

A few minutes later the information desk put Doctor Druse on the line where he confirmed his earlier diagnosis. They had sealed off the bleeder and restored blood flow, his cautious diagnosis was for full recovery to the eye. While we were sitting praying over Bonnie, Doctor Mason joined us and woke our sleeping beauty.

He tested her reflexes in both hands, both feet, and asked her a few questions about herself. Some she answered readily, others after struggling to remember, and a few she looked at him blankly having no clue. With the exception of the events surrounding the actual accident, her short term memory seemed intact.

She had good recall of her time among us at the Widespot, people, places, and names. She remembered her childhood clearly, speaking of those events as if recent. She had no recall at all of her time spent in college or while living in Oregon.

When the nurse indicated we should let her rest, I took her hand and kissed her on the right cheek. She looked up, smiled and said, "I love you Bum." Nate caught me before I hit the floor.

Not really, but I stood there dumb founded, unable to respond. Nate finally said, "we love you too."

In the elevator on the way to the cafeteria I repeated her words, "I love you Bum." Nate smiled, "of course... we all love you Bum."

They let us back in to see her about 7:00, but just for a minute the nurse cautioned. She seemed tired and less coherent than before, but talked to us asking about Faith, Buffy and the girls. I got my nerve up just before we left and moved close to her again, kissed her cheek and told her my heart, "I love you too, Bonnie." She smiled, squeezed my hand, and closed her good eye.

PART THIRTEEN

Ten days, ten grueling days I had lived with fear and elation walking the peaks and valleys, in the sunlight and shadows, questioning God's sovereignty. Nate, Bonnie, and I were home now, at the Widespot, life returning to its routine. But our lives had been changed in an instant and forever.

There she sat at the counter talking and laughing with Mae, waiting for the morning crowd to arrive, looking for the most part like nothing had happened. Yes, she sported a scar on her abdomen, still walked tentatively without her usual vigor, and lacked knowledge of whatever pain she had suffered those years ago in Oregon that had caused her not to be open with me. However, with that gone, she had blossomed like a rose, open, willing to share her heart with me.

As October began, she and Mae chatted often like school girls planning for their upcoming wedding day. Nate and I stood by passively watching and smiling as they discussed and re-discussed detail after detail. We had agreed to make it a double wedding, choosing to participate in each others joy rather than compete.

Mark, Becky, and their two sons had agreed to drive down from Canada to perform the ceremony for us when Pastor Jamison had been unable to do so. Bonnie and I had made plans to return to Canada with them, making reservations in Jasper for our honeymoon.

At Sunday's service we had announced our plans to marry to the congregation. We had thanked them for their prayers for Bonnie and asked for prayer as we followed God into whatever he had planned for us. Buck, of course, had stood and asked who would be cooking for the reception. Buffy then stood also and took a bow amid smiles and cat calls. It felt that we'd been through the fire, I could almost still smell the smoke in my hair, but we had survived and were stronger for it.

It appeared that I'd soon be out of work and Bonnie without a place to stay. She would be replaced by the new groom at Mae's house and I by Buffy, to whom Mae and I had given the Widespot Café. Our little church had new carpet and would have, God willing, extra pews to accommodate our guests by the 7th.

I had read somewhere once an apt description... 'the world is our oyster'. That is the view I held of the future Bonnie and I will make together, of an oyster to be opened with the possibility of finding a precious pearl inside.

"Good morning, welcome to the Widespot Café, can I get you a cup of coffee? Let me tell you about......"

– THE END –

For a good long time, Bum and I breathed the same air, he seasoned my roast beef and I cried while chopping his onions. While my heart pumped his blood, his heart gave me inspiration and faith. ~ dan

Author's note:
When the author's tears mix with the printer's ink, there may be value to his reader far beyond the printed word.

– DANisms –

- A heart filled with love is easily led, but a heart filled with bitterness and scorn remains deceitful...

- Punishment without love is not justice but retribution, little is learned from it by the offender except to be more stealthy and not be caught...

- Punishment for offense is necessary and proper and must be exacted, but take care that the purpose is to edify the offender and not to glorify oneself...

- For one to learn from error, punishment must be followed up with love and respect, allowing the offender to be humble and ask for forgiveness...

- Mistakes are building blocks and can be stepping stones to success or millstones around our necks, bringing only despair without understanding. Repent and grow from error...

- If God has trouble teaching, correcting, and growing man, how can man expect to do better?

- Relationship not based upon trust, love, and respect is doomed to fail...

- We are poor judges of ourselves, but humility will open our eyes...

- What if God said, "Aha! I have caught you" each time you made a mistake? Would you not give up? But instead, He is gentle with recrimination and uses the rod sparingly, but love lavishly...

- It is not the deed itself, but its intent that more aptly describes it's value.

- There are NO disposable people, not the old, the infirm, the young, disabled, or the unborn... they are all God's creation.

- What guides your heart, guides your hands, what your hands produce is a testimony to the fruit of the Spirit within you.

- Even if you pick only the worthy one, there are too many challenges facing us each day, too many battles to fight, too many wrongs to right. Let God guide you to the place where your efforts will be blessed and multiplied, as were fishes and loaves.

– AVAILABLE NOW –
The Cady Miller Series

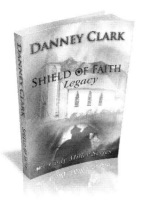

SHIELD OF FAITH - *Legacy*

"One more thing, Red, then if you want I'll shoot you, okay? Thing is, if you should beat me, I go to Heaven to be with the Lord, but if I beat you, where do you suppose you'll go for all eternity? Have you thought about how long forever in Hell might be?"

Red cursed again. "You don't worry about me miner, you worry about your little family here after I shoot you!"

SHIELD OF HONOR

Amid the explosions and aerial displays that marked our nation's Independence Day, he heard a yell followed by a louder and sharper report that was closely followed by a second and third. Cady, in his blue uniform with Kevlar vest and duty belt, was lifted off his feet by the impact and fell fifteen feet from the pier into the East River.

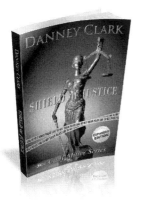

SHIELD OF JUSTICE - *Expanded*

Unknown to others, Cady Miller was a dangerous man, having the physical and technical abilities to inflict mortal injury. His lean stature and rapidly advancing age belied his physical prowess. His pale blue eyes now retained their 20/20 vision by the use of contacts lenses, but more importantly he used that vision to see things others often missed. Skills honed through years of training and discipline allowed him to maintain an edge others frequently lost as the years caught up with them.

These and other offerings available at the Author's website:
www.danscribepublishing.com

– AVAILABLE NOW –
The Cady Miller Series

BORN TO SERVE

He abandoned his sniper rifle and buried it with his military issued boots, his pack, and clothing in the ground beneath a large cholla cactus that stood alone near a singular formation of rocks. From his pack he took only dirty and well-worn local clothing, a tattered sombrero, and a pair of shoes that had been specially made for him, while leaving behind his radio and .45 semi-auto.

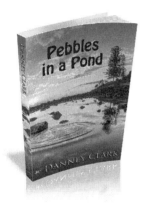

PEBBLES IN A POND

Hebrews 9:27 says, "And just as it is appointed for man to die once, and after that comes judgment." With that in mind, my character Cady Miller, like Lazarus or those who rose from their graves following Jesus' crucifixion (see Matthew 27: 51-53) are eternal beings still living on earth. While they will each physically die, they return again do the works which God calls them to do over and over until Christ returns.

These and other offerings available at the Author's website:

www.danscribepublishing.com

– AVAILABLE NOW –

THE EVER PRESENT STORM

Nestled in the mountains of Utah, a few miles east of Provo, is a little village of no more than a thousand people properly named Eden.

Unknown to its mortal inhabitants, angels and others walk among them, waiting for assignments from God to interact for good. I would wonder if there has always been a place like this somewhere on earth where good has made its home.

JELLY BEANS

Within the cover of this little book are well over two dozen short stories and not unlike jelly beans, while distinctly different, they are at the same time similarly pleasing to the eye, colorful, and delicious to enjoy.

ODDS & ENDS

God's perfect plan includes memory. Memory is God's way of allowing us to relive events in our lives. We learn and grow from our mistakes, our poor choices, and take joy and inspiration from those which were right and in which we can be proud as we relive them. This collection of Odds & Ends are those things He has brought to mind and which I chose to share with my readers. Praise be to God for allowing me to share them.

These and other offerings available at the Author's website:

www.danscribepublishing.com

– AVAILABLE NOW –

Chronicles of the
WIDESPOT CAFÉ

After college, nine years went by quickly, I moved from job to job, town to town, never having a close relationship or a feeling of belonging. I worked in every industry, every position, in every field garnering small success but feeling alone and empty inside.

To my credit, I lived on my earnings, not touching my investments, but spending all that I made. I drove taxi, waited tables, painted houses, sold shoes, installed computers, cooked, drove truck, did construction, or whatever came along.

Young, healthy, and able to learn quickly, I was easily employable. I have never owned a house, a car, or been married. Like King Solomon, I searched for the meaning of life, and like him, I didn't find it. I had many friends, none close, no ties, few responsibilities, felt no kinship to anyone except possibly the friend and partner I knew in college. But he had now moved on and marched to a different beat.

Then one day I stopped by the Widespot Café intending to just have a meal... that day, it all changed for me. I met Mae and Jib.

ANTIQUES &
ANTIQUITIES

Sitting back a distance from the heavily traveled highway linking the northern and southern parts of the state stands a building which looks much like an old barn. The outside is weathered and has been added onto many times by its various owners who were not very discerning in the design.

A large collection of discarded remnants of the past adorn its mottled exterior, adding both a cluttered look and a certain charm.

If only they could talk...

These and other offerings available at the Author's website:

www.danscribepublishing.com

SPOONFULS FROM HEAVEN

This little book is much the same as a savory stew, made up of both large and small bites of various ingredients and with a dash of this here and a pinch of that there added for flavor.

Some readers will enjoy the texture and the flavor of the whole stew, while others may enjoy one ingredient more than another. Eaten as a meal, it is my prayer that you will find it both filling and satisfying.

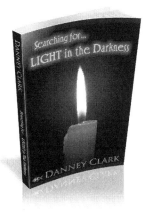

Searching for... LIGHT in the Darkness

Often we forget how great our God really is, by letting the fallen world overwhelm us and take away our joy. We should recognize that God created the world in the image of Himself, perfect and without sin. Man, then, through his disobedience, opened the door to the sin about which these pages tell.

Pay special attention to *Cremains* and recognize that the GOD who is great enough to create mankind is also great enough to forgive mankind and return him once again to perfection.

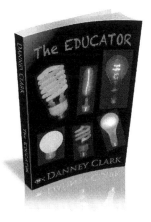

The EDUCATOR Six Bright Bulbs

A U.S. History teacher chooses six over-achievers and challenges them to choose a person outside of their family who they feel represents a taste of America's past, then to write a biography of that person for a pass/fail semester grade.

– AVAILABLE NOW –

KEYS TO YOUR HEART

While *Keys to Your Heart* is uniquely different than the original *Spoonfuls from Heaven* in content, they are very much alike in that they portray everyday life and showcase the result of our choices when dealing with life's challenges.

Each story has been specifically written for ages from late elementary through adult. The author suggests that parents of young children read these stories to determine in advance which stories they deem suitable for their own children.

DEADLY BUTTERFLIES

If there were such a thing as deadly butterflies, what would they be? Would they sting like bees or would they carry disease and infection like flies, would they eat meat like wasps or draw blood like mosquitoes?

What are the **Deadly Butterflies** in your life... food, drink, drugs, money, fame, sex, or status? What desirous and seemingly harmless thing lures you to its beauty, then tempts you to capture it while looking fragile and innocent, all the while having the capacity to ruin and kill?

BODY PARTS

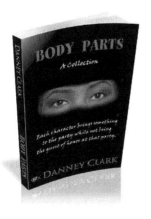

Just as the human body is made up of various parts with each having a vital function for the health and vitality of the whole, spiritually each God-created being who believes in Jesus as God is also a part of the Body of Christ and contributes to the health of the body of believers as well. Those who desire to understand may want to read 1 Corinthians Chapter 12. The enclosed stories will hopefully give some evidence of how each character takes something to the party while not being the **guest of honor** at that party.

These and other offerings available at the Author's website:

www.danscribepublishing.com

About the Author

Danney Clark is a third-generation Idahoan, businessman, husband and father. A Christian, a family man, and once an outdoorsman, hunter, and fisherman, he now finds contentment in working, writing, and attempting to understand life.

Married for more than 50 years to the same Idaho-born woman, he has two daughters, two granddaughters, and a great-granddaughter. He is enjoying his life to the fullest.

Danney Clark • 208-789-3034
www.danscribepublishing.com

I Aspire to Inspire!